SEDUCTION, DECEPTION, ILLUSION AND TRUTH

Photographs of pages 59, 111 and 159 has been reproduced by courtesy of Departamento Asuntos Taurinos de la Comunidad de Madrid.

Front cover: Derechazo or right-handed pass. César Rincón (p. 141)

© 2001 Ediciones Polígrafa, S.A.
Balmes, 54 – 08007 Barcelona – ventas@ed-poligrafa.es

© Photographs: Ricardo B. Sánchez
© Texts: José Luis Ramón, Rosa Olivares and Ricardo B. Sánchez
© Translation: Muriel Feiner and Richard Rees.

Layout: Estudio Polígrafa / B. Martínez

I.S.B.N.: 84-343-0947-5
Dep. legal: B. 5.587 – 2001 (Printed in Spain)

Color separation: Format Digital, Barcelona
Printing and binding: Mateu Cromo, Madrid

SEDUCTION, DECEPTION, ILLUSION AND TRUTH

A PHOTOGRAPHIC APPROACH TO BULLFIGHTING PASSES

PHOTOGRAPHS BY RICARDO B. SÁNCHEZ   TEXTS BY JOSÉ LUIS RAMÓN AND ROSA OLIVARES

EDICIONES POLÍGRAFA

CONTENTS

To Sarah, Ricardo and Alexandra

RICARDO B. SÁNCHEZ "To transmute the threatening and dangerous existence of a beast into something as gossamer as a dancer's veil, is the great marvel of bullfighting" (Manuel Chaves Nogales). Combining the knowledge of his craft with intelligence, willpower, courage and art, a bullfighter uses a cloth (cape and *muleta*) to lead, dominate, pass and kill a charging bull. The pass as it occurs in a bullfight can be regarded as a metaphoric representation of life as it occurs outside of the ring. My photographs illustrate how though all passes are the same — the bull must always pass — they are never equal. Like fingerprints and the steps we take in our lives, there are no two that are identical; the pass is that which forever comes and goes, without ever repeating itself.

We are the result of what we have been. In Western theology, when God created Adam and Eve and placed them in paradise, nature and the human being were one and the same: good and immortal. Unfortunately, in this story, evil took the form of a snake and an apple tree, both representing nature; thereby, Eve was seduced and Adam deceived. Paradise was lost and we were condemned to fear our mortality. Ever since, and leaving theological considerations aside, our relationship with nature has been ambiguous at best. Western culture has been involved in a power struggle with nature since we recognized it as the giver and taker of life.

Today, an ancient ritual continues wherein the human being plays the character of good and evil, female and male, predator and victim. The bullfighter, dressed effeminately with a costume suitable for a snake, uses a red cloth (apple) to deceive the bull and creates a powerful drama between life and death. The bull, both symbol of the male and nature, is irrationally seduced and deceived by the cloth. While it pursues the illusion of a target, the beast is condemned because it threatens us with it's power and physical strength.

As I understand it, energy is action. It can be naturally chaotic and unpredictable, thereby escaping our control, or something to which we can give order. We are obligated to act without guarantees but we seek the widest possible margin of safety for our actions. The bullfighter, in his solitary confrontation with the bull, seems always to ask this eternal question — what is it that happens or comes to pass in our lives, in death? With each pass, he attempts to demonstrate his ability to dominate, to control the measure of time and space as they converge with the energy of the bull. Confronted by the magic and the mystery of his existence, the bullfighter requires answers as to how to act in each pass; he must estimate the precise distance that separates life from death. What meaning can one find in life as death passes so near; or perhaps, one only finds truth in life when death is so close at hand?

There are five fundamental maneuvers in a bullfight and each has a very particular function. The bull is received into the ring with a cape, he is thus led to the horse, then the *banderillas* are placed and finally we have the passes executed with the muleta, which set up the bull for the kill. The maneuvers with the *garrocha* (lances used by a horseman to damage and weaken the bull's neck and shoulder muscles) and the *banderillas* (rounded dowels, 70 cm long with a harpoon-shaped steel tip placed as a pair on top of the withers of the bull) are used to sap the bull of his strength thereby transforming the execution of their art into physical punishment. The movements with the capes, the red *muleta* and the final kill or *suerte suprema* are those which represent deception and illusion as an art form. With the cape and the *muleta*, the bull is punished with nothing but a cloth to lead and touch it. Deceived in his spirited charge, he is thus dominated and eventually killed. I am more interested in the use of deception and illusion as an extension of our culture than in the art of physical punishment. Therefore, all my attention has been dedicated to the passes

and what they mean. It is the paradox of the pass that it never ceases to deceive as it reveals its truth.

If we think of the pass as a series of steps or something that happens upon which the bullfighter's very life depends, we see in it analogies to power and its absence, luck and destiny, what happens or passes with our emotions, what happens when we take risks, both rationally and irrationally, what happens or passes with our fear and courage, with the magic of the unknown. Eventually, in the bullfight, as in our lives, death will be the end. What happens before we reach that end is what makes life and the bullfight fascinating. Life and its intimate relationship with fate involve a continuous questioning of that which appears to be and that which really is. Is it really me or does it simply look like me? Fact or enigma.

To admit the fragile and vulnerable nature of the human body when exposed to danger, and to recognize the immensity of the risk whereby the unpredictable becomes predictable, is part of the essence and seduction of bullfighting. The bullfight explains the inexplicable just as passion for someone or something, or seduction by a magic incomprehensibly mysterious but real at the same time, heightens and stimulates our desire to live. Only rarely do the bull, bullfighter, spectators and weather synchronize in such a way that the ritual flows harmoniously, whereby bullfighting is experienced in the limits of the unknown. Contemplation of the sublime is a profoundly emotional and moving experience. However, for the most part, man kills the beast with a colorful spectacle for an excuse. It is a lust for conquest, which is consummated in the kill; the beauty of the fight is a means to an end, or is it?

In the bullfighting pass, the contrast between doubt and certainty is extreme. The bullfighter doubts his pass will deceive the bull, and is only certain of safety once the bull has passed. This process is repeated time and time again by the bullfighter, thus becoming a metaphor of the risk all human beings take in each step of our lives. Some of our actions are obviously more dangerous than others, so the measure between doubt and certainty regarding the outcome of our actions is proportionate to the risk involved. Why are we so afraid of the unknown, why do we fear the obscurity of death and all that which stimulates our anxiety concerning what is apparently uncontrollable? A bullfighter can feel great fear before he faces the bull. He is judging what he is going to do and whether he will be able to dominate and control the bull. This doubt is a fundamental part of the bullfighter's life and it illustrates the uncertainty of our existence. What happens, when in spite of what you want to happen, things happen, as they will? In order to balance the fear produced by the doubt and uncertainty of our actions, we are capable of generating willpower and courage to ascertain that our actions are correct. The bullfighter does this by projecting his ego or self-importance to the point of a radiant conviction that allows him to dominate and conquer the bull. The selfish role of "me first" which we are all capable of playing, becomes a catalyst to overcome our fear and motivate our courage to survive. Me first: this is a rule imposed by a society, which is made up of more or less self-interested individuals. We think of satisfying our needs, wants and pleasures, and as long as we get what we want, we waste little time thinking about how our actions may affect others. Even though our evolution has been shaped by the power of our intelligence, for the most part, our culture has manipulated the materials necessary for our survival without considering the consequences of such manipulation. It is possible that in this existential process, we are under the illusion that this is the height of civilization, or we are easily deceived and seduced by the comforts and security of a particular lifestyle. Individually and socially our actions have a selfish perspective, and we contemplate the concepts of living in harmony with nature or environmental balance as utopia. Though we are realizing that this behavior must be modified for the benefit of the planet and the future survival of our own species, we are still the great predators and no human being interprets this role better than the bullfighter. All good bullfighters must be very selfish; only in this way can they generate the necessary courage to face simultaneously the key roles of being possibly heroes or tragic victims of their unfortunate egotistical valor.

When a bullfighter enters the ring, he defies both the existential solitude of his life and his fear of dying. His actions in the bullring are a reflection of the solitude each human being encounters in confronting his existence. In his extreme and almost tragic isolation, the bullfighter knows that the spectators are all anxiously looking at him and yet none are capable of helping him if he is suddenly helpless before the bull. Alone, he is willing to overcome the fear of dying in order to feel the power and glory of his victory over death. It is for this reason that he is so admired, well paid and revered, for he is a bullfighter, confronting his solitude and fear, willing to risk his life for the glory of man, of all men. He is the last of the courageous hunters who risks all in order to kill, almost becoming a messiah-like figure, who by possibly sacrificing his existence, redeems the rest of us mortals from the sin of fear.

The creation of form, that which perpetuates our memory and endures, is a cultural attribute particular to the human species. Matter is manipulated to secure our survival and to glorify the memory of our existence. If death is the most visible and immediate expression of the disintegration of form, the desire to create form celebrates the will to live. In the process of creating a civilized world, mankind has used seduction, deception, illusion, and truth. This is especially so when it comes to establishing the codes which control and condition human behavior; codes such as religion, law, politics, economics, social status, etc. The fine arts also dwell in the ambiguous terrain of deception, seduction, illusion, and truth, for they lead us to

believe that by manipulating matter or concepts, we can create a concrete representation of life's multiple realities. Through our intelligence, knowledge and wisdom, we are capable of shaping the form of life itself. We are seduced by our ability to create form and regard judging the true or illusionary value of such a capability as a secondary consideration. If we consider an art form as something created by the human being, and we recognize our ability to shape life itself, then I consider that the most important art, is the art of knowing how to live. Because we must deal with reality before contemplating its interpretation, the art of living focuses on the immediacy of what we do with our lives. The fine arts on the other hand, are a sophisticated medium through which we express our feelings, thoughts and the implicit mysteries of our existence. Because it is so all encompassing, the art of living is the most difficult of all artistic disciplines.

Photography, as an extension of what we see and as a fine art, is a sophisticated expression and an extension of the art of living. The photographer chooses that which is important to him or her, thereby establishing a peculiar relationship between fascination with and conflict with what is being photographed in order to stimulate a worthy reflection of our existence. It seems evident that someone who photographs the tragedy of war, poverty or any other subject that is being personally investigated can be both attracted to and confused by what he or she photographs. In photography, as in life, there are many paths and each person must follow his own; thus seeing what I have seen and seeing what others have seen, I may learn to live a better life.

Bullfighting celebrates the domination and conquest of the fighting bull. It is a real and vital blood rite regardless of whether it is judged as good or evil. I am interested in the idea that we, as predators, kill to live and live to kill. Our intelligence allows us to manipulate, control and pretentiously attempt to dominate what we consider to be "nature", a "nature" which Western culture has always feared and admired because it is the giver and taker of life. Bullfighting is a ritual with a strict order imposed to simulate the principles of the eternal conflicts between life and death. The bull and bullfighter create a dance in which time, space and energy converge between light and darkness. My photographs record a reflection of this incomprehensible and passionate *pas de deux*, where the bull and bullfighter trace the lines and forms of their existence with each pass, confronting their lives with their destiny. As an investigation of the photographic language, these photographs are clearly a combination of what the eye can see as apparently real, and what can only be seen as a product of photographic technology. I have photographed the extensive variety of passes portraying the dialogue which occurs between that which moves and that which stays still, these photographs strive to illustrate the proper execution of the passes performed in the arena. These are images that suggest a relationship between the controllable and the uncontrollable, between what is apparently static and what is constantly moving.

From the beginning of my investigation in this subject, I have combined abstraction as a representation of the unknown with realism to represent what we recognize in order to suggest metaphors about the passing of our lives. The bullfighter creates that which instantly disappears in time; I have created photographs of that which we are incapable of seeing to celebrate his magic. Using the knowledge of how light can be reproduced, the photographer can create an illusion which represents an instant of reality frozen in time and defined in space by the boundaries of its own frame. My photographic process transforms the vision of what I see into a mirror from which I want to learn. This constant looking and reflecting reminds me of how difficult it is to see beyond the obvious, and how easily we are deceived and seduced by the illusion of what we think is real and true. While I do not condone or condemn bullfighting as a spectacle, I hope this book will reflect on the bullfighting passes as metaphors of the broader relationship between nature and us. I selected these photographs to reveal the essence of a sublime pass, to reflect the passing of light and darkness, which is the soul of this ritual.

CHANGE OF HANDS BEHIND THE BACK. CÉSAR RINCÓN. "LAS VENTAS". MADRID. 6-6-1991

THE ART OF PASSING AND LEAVING TRACES

What the Eye Cannot See

Between the certain and the uncertain, between certainty and doubt, there is a strange territory in which the senses are unable to guide us, in which light and darkness merge to create a blinding chiaroscuro. It is in this territory that intuition, desire, dream and illusion produce what are sometimes monsters, sometimes gods. It is also in this nameless place — and those who come so far and are not afraid to continue, despite the unstable terrain, know this — where art grows, where man justifies his existence, where we want to return in order to continue believing in innocence and truth.

We rely on our senses and we rely increasingly on technique and technology, a prolongation of our senses, of our body. What the eye cannot see can be captured by a camera. In situations where time is incalculably fast and events succeed each other without becoming defined as images, the lens may capture the beam of light that produces a gesture. Our trust in our senses as the only possible way to trap existence is now a theme for poets only. The definition of reality, of certainty, has changed to the point where it fades into thin air. Technology, the machine, exists to perfect perception, to go beyond what a man can reach with his hearing, with his sight. There are machines that can portray what we cannot see, not only making us doubt our own sensorial capacity but also altering the limits of what we consider real. There are cameras that, apparently, are able to capture the aura, that halo of heat all living bodies emit which has always been a symbol of holiness. The golden ring that religious painting has immortalised. But this symbol, this idea of saintliness is no longer this; now it is something completely different because we know that every living body has one. Furthermore, it is something that can be given visual form in a photograph. This knowledge may change our concept of what is real, make us doubt about what we believe

T. N.: *Pase*: the moment when the *torero* incites the bull to charge, then lets it pass by; *Faena*: the series of passes with the muleta; *Suerte*: fate or luck; *Suertes*: bullfighting maneuvers.

because we see it and what we do not believe because we cannot see or perceive it with our senses. Today we know that even DNA has a recognizable form, a photographically reproduced image. Today we know what we cannot see physically, but what we believe in with greater or lesser conviction acquires form; and suddenly, between what we can see and what we cannot see, barriers emerge not of truth, but of illusion.

Photography has transformed our concept of reality. Through its images we have reconstructed the idea of what is true and what is false, finally to realize that it is merely a prolongation of man's ability to continue creating an illusion. As a part of art, that cultural game that emerges from man's atavistic need to search for truth and to hide and disguise it to continue seeking it, in order not to find it, photography began with this search for truth to eventually collaborate in the construction of an illusion. For while in its origins photography was the documentation of objective reality, having evolved into a cultural tool it has reached the same point as all the other artistic languages: an illusion, a game of seduction and deceit that man himself constructs. Every photograph is undoubtedly a document of something; at least it is proof that the exact moment it preserves for posterity actually existed. That it happened, and that there was someone there with a camera to show that it happened. But what do these photographs by Ricardo Sánchez prove? They give no face to this man, to this bullfighter who risks his life, or to that other who makes a long, elegant *pase*. Naturally, some *aficionados* would be able to identify the *diestro*, or matador, by his body, by his gesture... but this is not what the photographer is after. These images may be proof that once again the ritual, the game of life and death occurred and that, once again, man defeated the animal. But no, what these photographs document is the images' ability to seduce, like beauty, colour and movement deceive the animal, like the sheen on a surface, a fleeting beauty, deceives us. Through our capacity to deceive we may even replace the natural with the artifical, nature with an indoor plant.

Light is the origin of colour, the essence of painting, the basis of photography. And deceit converges in light. These photographs are simply documenting deceit. The deceit that is produced around life and

death in the *fiesta* of the bulls. That absurd deceit that leads the bull to death chained to a blood-coloured *muleta*. It is the document of an abstraction that becomes tangible in real life and which fades away between light and movement in these photographs. An abstraction that is also a symbol. And this is what differentiates these photographs from so many others that highlight courage, ferocity, art, the body, the bullfight (as the Anglo-Saxons call it, an inadequate translation that nonetheless defines the *fiesta de los toros*). For this reason also, these photographs are far removed from the usual document to become a testimony, although still a document, that comes from somewhere else. It is also for this reason that the fascination of these works lies in a more conceptual rather than visual terrain. Although here Ricardo Sánchez uses the same seduction that he speaks to us about in his photographs. He also deceives us, makes us enter the cape, and it is here that we return to the bullfight, to the man-to-man struggle between the images we see and the ideas that occur to us as we contemplate them.

What attracts us about these photographs is not horror. It is their beauty that catches our eye, their color, the fleeting presence of the shadow of death, that vertigo produced when someone risks his life, or even something more. We have already been deceived. Seduced by illusion, deceived by appearances, attracted by beauty, we come to a place that was not announced. We thought we were looking at bullfight photographs, and suddenly we realise that there is no bullfighter and no bull, that what we were staring at and believed we were seeing, almost with the background noise of a bullring, is a deep well in which lights lead us to the density of a black stain. Caught up in a dance of colors we are guided, we discover that the gold and the lights are life, that the ring does not exist since its dimensions are infinite and therefore beyond the scope of the lens. We realise that there is no blood, nor words, that there are no spectators and that only rarely is there tragedy. There is only the shadow of death, the presence of danger like an aroma, like a color. And looking at these photographs we come to think of bullfighting as a collective performance, we realise that this magic ritual is what now, without religion, or sin, or blood, or death, is what surrounds certain artistic actions. Those in which the body is used as a work field, in which the idea of action is centered on the sublime quality of existence, on the infinite vulgarity of the things that make us revolve and move. We are reaching the point of searching for an explanation for what has no meaning other than the terrain of sensations, of rituals and of tragedies.

The idea of seduction is linked to illusion and deceit, like truth to lies, like good to bad, like bad to worse. The illusion of appearances, the illusion of the desired, of what we do not have, the deceit of appearances, of beauty, of youth. Eternal youth, the postponement of death to a later time. While young men dress as dancers and enter the ring to kill black bulls ten times their weight. To risk their lives in an ancestral rite. For neither the speed of a race track, nor the summit of a frozen mountain, nor the darkest chasm is the same thing. It is not the same thing. Not the same thing?

We are speaking of deceit, and art is undoubtedly the territory that best represents it. The art of bullfighting does so symbolically. On the other hand, literature does so in a mathematical, logical way: "What is life? An illusion, a shadow, a fiction. Everything in life is a dream and dreams... are no more than dreams", said Calderón de la Barca. Others deceived themselves in other ways, by swearing eternal love beyond the grave, perhaps as proof of absolute devotion or perhaps like that red cape with which the bullfighter deceives the bull, like the lover who seduces his loved one. Beyond life we shall merely be dust, "but enamoured dust", promised Francisco de Quevedo. Illusion and deceit, we said, come together, and there is no illusion like the one art produces. Painting, full of representation, of stories that substitute others, and finally photography, before cinema, the great deceit of appearances in the name of the purest truth, of the truth which is the product of technology, as nobody today would question.

Photography is true because everything that has been photographed existed. But everything that serves to speak the truth serves equally to speak the opposite, such as words. And fiction, that is, illusion, dream, comes with the word. Photography, like all the media that man has invented to express himself, was born from the intention of transmitting experiences and sensations, of giving form to dreams and desires. But these methods have evolved rapidly and have adapted to form, to the nature of the human race, and they have become new forms of deceit, of creating illusion, of concealing and transforming, to deceive and lie with what has always been a principle of credibility. Photography is the paradigm of the reliable document, and it is also a technique that may be manipulated, assembled, deprived of meaning to produce something that is not real despite its appearance of reality. Art is approached in this way, that magic device with which man tells his own tale, deceives and ennobles himself, with that form of being more human, of turning defects into virtues, of analysing and delving into every recess of the mind and the unconscious. If we expect truth from photography, we are deceiving ourselves. The truth can be only in our gaze. If from photography we expect explanations, the perfect image that clarifies the situation, we must look in another way or perhaps elsewhere. Deceit, the game of illusions, appearances, these are all the subject matter of art. For this reason, it has developed its vast symbolic capacity, its psychological depth, because man deceives and seduces, but eventually even in his forms of deceiving, flashes of truth may appear. Or at least of that truth of his being, of that way of wanting to be. Intention and intuition invariably emerge from behind a more or less successful act of deceit. Illusion always becomes truth. Or perhaps it is another illusion.

When photography has taken the bullfight as its subject, the resulting works have been very disparate, although most of them eulogize the magic and beauty of a pagan festival beyond time and place. The colors, the bodies, sex permanently in a latent foreground, death and danger and, above all, beauty and spectacle. Only few have seen anything else, perhaps because they did not want to see anything else. Between relating what is outside and investigating what remains inside exists the same difference as between art and the graphic document, between speaking about what is private and establishing universal principles lies the development of artistic creation.

The series *Pases*, which Ricardo Sánchez has been compiling for years all over Spain, attending bullfights in many rings and following individual bullfighters over entire seasons is not, curiously, a series of photographs of bulls, about bulls. It is not just that. Ricardo Sánchez has constructed a beautiful metaphor of life and, above all, of deceit. In his previous series, and in the occasional subsequent one, the idea of deceit, of the seduction that external forms exercise on us by concealing with their sheen and their outward appearance the true reality of their essence, constitutes the guideline, and it is in this series on the bullfight that he has come across, perhaps unexpectedly, the most complete and the most spectacular form of this deceit. A deceit that in the case of the bullfight leads straight to death, although risk and the pure game of seduction are the facets that bear most similarity to life, with its permanent games of deceit, of seduction, of adornment of appearances, that double public and private stance. Life leads inevitably to death, but who cares about this when in the middle of a game of seduction? Just like the bullfighter who does not stop to think about death when he makes a brilliant *pase* with his *muleta*, nobody wants to stop to see what lies behind that shining surface, apparent beauty, morning glory, perfect deceit by which we are taken in like the bull, blinded by the shine of blood, overcome by the yearnings of desire.

Magic and religion fill our memory with illusion, with rituals, and with deceits of seduction. The history of mankind, of culture, is marked by attempts at and achievement of deceit and seduction. Fables, legends, fragments of history whose intention is to create an illusion, characters who seduce us with deceit, with the ignorance that time and lack of information reinforce. And magic rites whose origins are lost in memory and all that remains of them is game, spectacle. Of all the primitive rituals only the bullfight, the art of *el toreo*, is still alive in the 21st century. And only in those restricted areas where the bull, a mythical animal, symbol of strength and virility, is still bred exclusively for the *Fiesta*.

In Spain, the bullfight is more than a spectacle, more than a tradition. It is part of a culture rooted in the deepest of all places: language. Bullfighting terms impregnate a language that contains words that cannot be translated into any other tongue, perhaps because they tell of feelings and situations that can be understood only from difference, from the ability to see the other side of appearances. And this needs time, time to sit down and watch how a man dressed in red and gold performs a dance of sex and death with a black animal ten times his weight. Time to understand that this is no macabre spectacle, that the bull is not martyred, for the animal is administered the noblest of deaths, the fight, in which it is given the chance to reveal its courage, its strength. It is true that the bull practically never kills the bullfighter (although this sometimes happens), and it is practically impossible that the bull's life will be spared and the animal allowed to return to the meadow with the wounds received in a struggle far more noble than the miserable death by machines in an abattoir. Time to feel that we are spectators of a symbolic dance, not just a man and a bull but something more, a metaphor of life, a masked ball in which we do not know who is disguised. Time to realise that everything is a deceit, and that with what we see we can construct only half a reality that needs the two sides, light and shade, life and death, joy and pain.

In life, as the poet said, "everything passes and everything remains, but we are doomed to pass...". In the bullfight, the *faena is built up on the basis of pases*. The verb *pasar* is a curious verb in Spanish. It is charged with innuendoes and it would be impossible to list all its possibilities here (something that no translator would forgive me for), but it is an essential term in the bullfight, just as it is essential to know the two basic laws: command and temper. One must know how to command the bull and to firmly withstand its charges. It is a conflict of characters rather than of bodies. And although we know that l ife is full of *cornadas* (gorings), we strive to believe that the bullfight is something else, merely a spectacle. We forget that in life, too, we must remain firm, show moderation, "withstand the charges" of all kinds.

Those who have seen a bullfight first hand will not easily forget the anxiety of the spectators: the color of the arena, the red blood, the gaze of the *torero*, the impression we get that the bull is an innocent victim, and though it is a foreseeable death — that of the bull — something else is in the air. It is life that parades before us, in those young, tense bodies, it is life as a game. An afternoon at the bullfight is a compendium of the life we lead, although we are unaware of this. It is an abbreviated catalogue of so many things in our lives that we never think about. Most probably because we do not have the time.

In Spain, language unwittingly returns time and time again to the ritual of the bulls, and not only in sayings and word plays. It is the essence that persists, and in the background of the bullfight, as in the background of myths, what remains is deceit. The bull is deceived from the very moment it enters the ring: the running, the colors, the punishment, the noise, the body of the bullfighter, so fragile and yet so imposing, involve the bull in a continuous dance until it meets its final *suerte*. *Suerte*! The *suertes* in bullfighting are the different phases of the *faena*, and before he enters the ring, everybody wishes the *torero suerte*. And if the fight goes badly, it is because *suerte* abandoned him. In life, too, if things go well or badly this apparently has more to do with *suerte* than with anything else. But the truth is elsewhere, and it has more to do with the permanent deceit with which we adorn our lives, our private *faenas*. Just as the bull is deceived, until it is killed, with a seduction of colours and blood in which apparently it always has a chance of salvation, in life everything may be an illusion, a shadow, fiction.

It is said that in the bullfight everything is deceit, except the courage of the bullfighter, and the strength and danger of the bull: except that life and death are at stake. The man, the *torero*, looks like a woman: the color of the *muleta* and the cape is not blood red, it is another color we see in them. Today, even the *torero*'s pigtails is false. The horses are heavily protected and they cannot pursue the bull, the sword the bullfighter carries as he engages in the *faena* is almost invariably sham... until the end. Until the end, nobody knows for certain what is true and what is false. It is said that the bullfight is a dance, a sexual dance, but this is another deceit, that thrill is pure illusion, or perhaps it is the thrill one feels in the face of maximum risk. It is true that the man-woman, the *torero*, dressed in sequins, dances before

the bull, almost invariably black, serious and armed, to deceive the beast, like an odalisque that leads it to the abattoir.

But the bullfight is much more than a road to death, it is the symbol of many things, not only of life as something absolute. It is also a parody of masculinity, the mass of disguised appearances.

We must know how to look in order to see beyond what the eye registers. Beyond the possibilities of our gaze lie not only the origin of light but also a world of impossible images. Since its invention, photography has become a witness of reality, of that moment that undoubtedly existed because we have its image, a photograph, the document of its reality, its existence. And this photograph is also proof that the moment no longer exists, that it passed. Photography thus becomes a document of the passage of time and, inexorably, of the reality of death. How many photographs confront us with those who are gone forever, with the feeling that they are no longer with us, and even with ourselves, in photographs that show us not the way we are today but the way we were and will never be again. It is like the image of a body without a shadow, a document that preserves something of the magic of its creation, of the impossibility of stopping time forever, even if only on a fragment of paper.

The photographs that Ricardo Sánchez has taken on so many afternoons of *fiesta*, of glory and of blood, are not the record of anything concrete in itself. On the one hand, they are a catalogue of the almost infinite types of *pases* in the bullfight, but this is merely a justification. In these photographs there is no anecdote, there is nothing more than the confrontation between light and darkness. In these images, like flashes of a fleeting existence, we are offered the fragment we never managed to see, that line of death hanging from the bull's horn. We see the black shadow, a formless stain, which is the bull as it charged, and we see the sequins of the *traje de luces* like little bells that almost chime. Unlike what usually happens in bullfight photographs, here there is no flesh, what there is is spirit. Behind these stains of color lies something more than an imagined body behind a shadow. In these photographs we see danger, we see deceit as if it were something physical, embodied. It may be glimpsed behind a flash of color, of light which makes the reddish yellow of the arena the perfect backdrop to the black of a bull that for an instant was death. And between life and death *pases* succeed each other, the afternoon passes and the game of deceit comes to an end once again in the bullring. But outside, in that other spectacle in which we are all *toreros*, although some would prefer to see the bulls behind the barriers, the risk of finding life continues. Deceit continues, but this time there are no elegant *pases* nor graceful gestures.

Translated by Richard Rees

To Mercedes

JOSÉ LUIS RAMÓN   **REGARDING SUERTE AND THE SUERTES***

The most frequently repeated word in bullfighting circles is "*Suerte*", meaning Luck, probably because, in his profession, the bullfighter is continuously flirting with death. The matador is wished "*Mucha suerte*" (Best of luck) when he is about to face the bull; he complains: "*No he tenido suerte*" (What bad luck I've had!) when things did not go well, or, to the contrary, "*Vaya suerte*" (What good luck!), if he has had the good fortune to encounter a good bull and was able to do well with it. A more technical phrase would be : "*Ponle en suerte*" (Get the bull into position), the matador's instructions to his *banderillero*, when he wants the bull placed in a specific area of the ring. "*Está fuera de la suerte*" (He is way out of line) is the typical reproach from the stands, directed at the bullfighter, if he is standing too far away from the animal or in an inappropriate terrain or distance. *Suerte* definitely seems to be the word to keep in mind when viewing the bullfight.

However, the word "*suerte*" indicates many more concepts, which are substantially different from the foregoing ones and which are what the reader will encounter most frequently in the course of this text. "*Suerte*" is the word used to refer to each and every one of the maneuvers performed during the course of the *lidia* or fight of each bull, regardless of whether the cloths — the big magenta and gold *capote* or cape, or the smaller red *muleta* —, are employed as long as a deliberate effort is made to *burlar* — trick or deceive — the animal. In fact, the term *Suertes del Toreo* is used to refer to the full range of cape and muleta passes, *lances* (specifically, cape passes), and *recortes* (maneuvers employed by the torero to abruptly cut off the bull's charge), as well as any other actions, with or without the use of any capes or lures, which the *lidiador* or bullfighter might employ in order to *torear* the bull. However, even though the *lance* and the *pase* are *suertes*, they are not quite the same thing: *lances* are the set of *suertes* which are performed with the cape, and the Spanish word *pases* refer to all those executed with the *muleta*. In English, we tend to use the word "passes" indistinctly for cape and *muleta* work, but, in Spanish, one would not say *muleta lances,* nor cape *pases.* Furthermore, there are other *suertes*, in which a *capote* or *muleta* are not present, such as the *suerte* of the *banderillas* (the meter-long barbed sticks placed in the bull's back) and the *suerte de varas* or picing phase.

In an effort to have the reader identify and associate the different *suertes* included in this book more easily, only those which have their corresponding photographic references will be written in *italics* lettering within the text.

* *Suerte*: luck; *Suertes*: bullfighting maneuvers.

One of the very first moves the bullfighter may decide to make can easily be termed a veritable "voyage into the unknown". The matador will slip out from behind the *barrera* fence and march ceremoniously across the entire ring, until he comes to a solemn halt before the *toril* gate, where he will fall to his knees in order to await the bull's entrance into the arena. This is probably the longest and most dramatic moment in the entire bullfight... those 10 to 12 seconds which it takes the matador to make his way to the *toril* gate (the door through which the bull enters the ring), cape in hand, and heart pounding wildly in his chest. The steps the torero takes in order to position himself to execute a *larga cambiada a porta gayola* represents a "voyage to the unknown", because no-one, absolutely no-one, knows what is going to happen when the long, black shadow of the bull emerges from the *chiqueros* (bull pens) and makes its entrance into the ring. It might just happen that the bull will appear on the sand, fix its sights immediately on the cape, and instinctively follow its movement, as a result of which, the *suerte* or *lance* will prove to be clean and effective. However, it might also charge out of the dark passageway into the bright sunlight, in a distracted manner, looking all over, glancing from one side to the other, sniffing the wind blowing across the sand, and due to that strange behaviour, it might fail to obey the matador's subtle commands with the cape. If that is the case, anything could happen; the animal could smash into the bullfighter, leap over his body, or totally ignore the kneeling figure before it, whose only protection will be his relatively flimsy pink and yellow cape.

The *larga a porta gayola* (or long, changed pass executed directly in front of the *toril* gate) and the path the torero takes until he reaches the *puerta de chiqueros* (that long tunnel from which the bull will emerge from the depths of the bullring, into the bright sunlight of the arena), can be considered a perfect metaphor of the true meaning of *Toreo* (or Bullfighting), and even of life itself. Bullfighting must be understood as an interminable trip into the unknown, which not only involves the certain death of the animal and the possible death of the man, but it also represents a continuous search for the bull's bravery, its noble nature, and its potential liberation following a brave and honest performance. For that very reason, no-one in his right mind goes to the bullring with the sole purpose of seeing the bull die, much less to relish in the blood spilled or the proverbial suffering of the animal; rather one goes to the ring seeking to savor the true essence of *toreo*, the profound art of bullfighting, and as a

result, the physical redemption of the bull and the spiritual redemption of the bullfighter, who skillfully submits the savage ferocity of the animal, to the point where he becomes a true hero in the eyes of the spectators. Therefore, even though the Fiesta can be called bloody — for indeed blood is spilled —, it is not cruel and the maximum reward granted to the brave bull can be the pardoning of its life and its salvation from death. This is a reward which is not without its religious significance, for it is one which neither all the bulls, nor even all of us humans are destined to attain. It might appear to be incongruous, that in a Fiesta in which so many bulls end up dying by the end of the year, that aficionados really go to the ring with the hope of being able to pardon the life of one, which has proven itself worthy. And it is the very spectators themselves who request that this maximum honour be granted to a brave bull in the course of the bullfight, an event and an experience which is as individual and subjective, as it is collective.

The true importance of the *larga a porta gayola* lies in the bull's unpredictable irruption into the arena and in its reaction to its violent clash with the light of day, after spending several hours in the semi-darkness of the bullring pens. And therein lies the true merit of the matador in this maneuver: the fact that he is dealing with an unknown entity, granting the bull all the advantages of the situation and even voluntarily relinquishing his own capacity to defend himself. The torero made the decision to execute this *suerte* (or maneuver), in the solitude of the *burladero*, while observing how the bullfighter, whose performance preceded his, is being either warmly applauded or totally ignored by the public, depending upon the success of his *faena*. It is called a *larga* or long pass, because the torero holds the cape in one hand, while releasing the other side of the cloth in order to make it flare out over his head. It is a ponderous decision indeed, because once the matador has taken the first step towards the *chiqueros*, there is no turning back. It is hard to imagine anything more ridiculous than a matador who changes his mind half-way along. I am sure that that no-one has ever done that in all bullfighting history, because it would represent the ultimate failure and very likely put an immediate and disgraceful end to his professional career.

The torero makes the decision to execute a *larga cambiada a porta gayola*, in a fraction of a second, and it is like a personal challenge, which the man poses first to himself, and then, to his colleagues and to the general

public. The matador who kneels down in front of the *toril* gate before it is opened and who is able to endure those agonising few seconds, which transpire before the bull makes its spectacular appearance in the ring, is displaying if nothing else, his steadfast courage and determination. However, it is not just a matter of bravery, because this *larga* is not a maneuver performed exclusively by the more valiant toreros, but rather it is a cape *lance* employed by highly determined matadors, who want to make it very clear to the spectators that they are going to do everything in their power to triumph.

In the end, the *suerte* could go well or not, because when the bull enters the ring, there are no hard nor fast rules, which can be applied, and everything will depend upon the skill, knowledge and fortune of the torero, always in equal proportions. Therefore, what should be evaluated, above and beyond the perfection of the *suerte*, is the fact that the man has simply decided to perform it. The torero who is capable of captivating, delighting and intimidating his audience with the way he drops to his knees, extends his cape and waits stoically for the bull to appear, in order to take control over it and lead it, with his daring and wild gestures, to where he wants it to go... The bullfighter who manages to do all of this, will win over the public. Afterwards, the *faena* may be long or short, memorable or forgettable, but something indelible will always remain, if the torero has executed a *larga a porta gayola*. Therein lies the truth about the way the torero chooses to confront the drama of bullfighting, and the still greater truth of his making a difficult decision, one of the most complicated that he will ever have to make during the corrida, and of having maintained his sense of dignity until the very end.

As is the case in almost all of the *suertes* in Bullfighting, the execution of the *larga cambiada* admits a series of variations, all of them very similar to one another, which, depending upon the moment or the way in which they are executed, will be of greater or lesser merit. The fundamental variation of the *larga a porta gayola* is the *larga cambiada en el tercio* (the area between the *barrera* fence and the circle painted on the sand). It is executed once the bull has entered the ring and has made a turn or two of the arena, carried along by its own initial impetus. In this *suerte*, the bullfighter also falls to his knees and releases the cloth with one hand, while swirling it over his head, fully extended with the other. However, between one *larga* and another, there is one fundamental

difference: the fact that he can change his mind in this latter version at the very last minute and no-one will know the difference. This apparently minor distinction, which may seem insignificant — the possibility of not executing the kneeling *larga* pass, if the bull seems to be reacting strangely, or, to the contrary, deciding to execute it if he discovers that the animal is a straight charging one —, is what turns one *larga* into a true and honest accomplishment and the other, into just one of the many recourses and adornments which the torero can employ during the *lidia*.

This type of *larga* is called a *cambiada* or changed pass because the bull's charge is initially directed to one side (for example, along the right flank, which is the hand holding the cape, while the other one only serves to attract the animal's attention), but it is finally switched to the opposite side, thus obliging the animal to change the course of its charge. That is, a change is imposed on the bull's charge. In fact, in many *suertes* of bullfighting, a similar change is impressed upon the bull, especially in the *tercio de banderillas* and in some of the maneuvers with the *muleta*. However, the *largas* (that is, the action of releasing the cloth with one hand and only using the other to guide it) obviously correspond exclusively to the work with the cape. As we have seen, a *larga* can be the bullfighter's very first intervention in the *lidia* (he can perform them either kneeling opposite the *chiqueros* or beside the circular lines drawn on the sand), and they can also be employed as receiving *lances*, performed standing up by the *banderilleros*. It is important to point out a significant distinction, in that the *largas de rodillas* do not embody many of the fundamental concepts of bullfighting: aesthetics do not come into play in this *suerte*, nor does the concept of *temple*, much less that of *poder* or domination. In the *largas de rodillas* there is only fearless audacity and an evident determination to triumph, but there is still no profound *toreo*.

The bull emerges from the *chiqueros* with power and nobility and barring extreme cases of debility, maintains all of its natural strength intact, and so, it will have to be brought around and under control. To *parar* or stop the bull is the expression used by the toreros, which means precisely that: to force it to stop running around so that it can be fought in a profound and aesthetic fashion. It is still a strong animal, without a shadow of a doubt, but it is no longer a "gadabout", running around wildly. Consequently, the "receiving" passes are extremely important, for they form the repertoire used by the matador or *banderillero* to determine what the bull is like, to stop it, to

subdue it and to teach it to charge. Within this group of *suertes* we cannot include the kneeling *largas de rodillas*, which are really just flashes of courage and daring do on the part of the torero, who feels that before getting down to the basics of *toreo*, he must first seduce the spectators and create in them an illusion of fear and valour. And for that reason, the moment immediately prior to the execution of the *larga a porta gayola* is so important — the moment of maximum determination —, because once this pass is executed, what is left are just the "fireworks", which take advantage of the bull's drive and the momentum, but the real, pure *toreo* will come later.

Profound *toreo* will make its appearance in the receiving passes: standing *largas* (which only the banderilleros really employ), moving cape passes (done only when necessary, indistinctly by the matador or by his *subalternos* or assistants) and, most especially, it appears in the *verónicas*. Here, in the leading *suerte* of cape fighting, there is control, and, above all else, a great deal of truth, as long as it is executed correctly.

The *verónica* represents the ultimate in cape fighting, its most sublime form of expression. And perhaps, its maximum difficulty as well. Performing *verónicas* is not difficult for a professional, but performing good *verónicas* only falls within the realm of a chosen few. Throughout the history of Tauromachy, there have been a handful of *maestros* who have recorded their names in letters of gold in the "Annals of *Toreo*", merely because they were magnificent executors of the *verónica*. This *suerte* is called thus, because the cape is presented directly before the bull, supposedly in the same manner that Saint Veronique, according to the Bible, used the holy shroud to wipe the sweat and blood from Christ's face. The *verónica* demands from the bullfighter a conciliation of elements which are very difficult to bring together within the very brief span of time of its execution. In the *verónica*, there is no more demonstration of valor than that which is absolutely necessary in order to move the cape slowly and hold one's ground, withstanding the bull's charge rushing past one's stomach and without moving one's feet a single centimetre. Obviously, all of this requires a great deal of valor, to say the very least. A good *verónica* features infinite *torería* and constitutes a magnificent display of how the matador must co-ordinate all the movements of his body: those of his waist, chest, arms, shoulders, hands, wrists, legs, head, chin... He must adapt the movements of his entire body to those of the *capote*, which is being dragged along the ground as if it had wings and a life of its

own, with immense depth and feeling, and he must do all of this while the bull brushes against the fine embroidery of his suit of lights. A good *verónica* must be executed slowly, the slower the better, with the bullfighter treading into the bull's terrain, because a good *verónica* must be like a sudden outburst of creative inspiration, which runs through the torero from head to toe, and through the bull, from right to left.

As a result, it is very difficult to fight *a la verónica* well, and for that very reason, the torero who possesses the necessary grace and good fortune to do so (or perhaps we should call it "art, genius and spirit") is respected as if he were some sort of pagan god or taurine monarch. Most of these "kings of the *verónica*", that select group of *diestros* who have elevated this bullfighting *suerte* to the maximum artistic category, are of gypsy origin, although no-one knows why the gypsy toreros seem to carry in their genes all the grace, elegance and art required to perform the *verónica* well. We can make special mention of "Cagancho", "Curro Puya", "Gitanillo de Triana", Rafael Albaicín, and "Rafael de Paula", the most recent of all of them, and also the only one I have been able to see perform. "Paula" is a torero who despite his physical impotence and at times, apparently moody indifference, has performed *verónicas* precisely the way we aficionados dream they should be done.

However, of course, not all the *verónicas* achieve such a highly stylistic category. There are, in addition to the sublime *verónicas*, good ones and bad ones, correct ones and dutiful ones, all of them performed in accordance with the properly established geometric rules of *toreo*. No-one can criticise their execution, among other reasons, because they form the immense majority of what we are likely to see in the bullrings today.

In addition to the *verónica* as such, which has a pure, aesthetic content, the more authentic, the better it is executed, there are other *verónicas* which try to add a dramatic touch to the fundamental *suerte*: *verónicas with one knee on the ground*, or sometimes, even both, which is certainly more difficult, and, as a result, less graceful and attractive. The toreros who use these different variations of such a classic *suerte*, do so with the idea of winning over the spectators, captivating them and showing them that what others do on foot, they are capable of doing on their knees. It does not matter that in order to do so, they must sacrifice a certain amount of plasticity in the process, for, in the end, the *suerte* becomes far more difficult and dangerous. We will be seeing, as we explain step

by step the different *suertes* of *toreo,* that all of the passes executed on foot in accordance with the most classic codes, can also admit a kneeling version, or a variation performed with a half cape, with the cape held behind the matador's back, or gazing up at the stands, which is equivalent in some way to "looping the loop" of *Toreo*, in a constant search for the "most difficult feat yet". With these more daring interpretations, the matador seeks to show the spectators that he is willing to risk his life cleanly and assume all the dangers involved in what he is doing.

As a result, then, we can speak of *verónicas* executed with one or both knees on the ground, which are extremely difficult, because it is not easy to react in such an uncomfortable position in the event that the bull should behave strangely. We have already pointed out that these *verónicas* are, in the broadest sense of the word, receiving *lances*, and are used to slow down and submit the bull.

In order to execute a *verónica*, the torero stands with his feet apart (adopting an open stance), at the same time that he bends slightly at the waist. There is also another *verónica,* which is performed with feet together, which is then called *lance a pies juntos*, marking just a simple nominal distinction. These *lances* are receiving maneuvers, which are often used with bulls showing a short charge or limited strength, because holding one's hands up high proves to be less punishing for them, and makes it possible to fight animals which would otherwise not admit a deep, pure and low *verónica*. If the torero offers the bull his profile instead of his chest, they are called *lances de costadillo* and if the cape is held close to his body, they are *delantales* (apron passes), as if the *capote* were a kitchen apron. In time, the *delantales* have progressed from aggressive passes, intended to control and submit a violent bull, to smooth *lances* which try to coax a more docile animal to charge.

Lances with feet together, in contrast with the more renting execution of the *verónica*, are deemed lighter and more superficial, although this does not mean that they are less elegant and entail less *torería*. Both versions are considered fundamental *suertes,* which the matador uses with two major goals in mind: one is the desire to do well and be warmly applauded by the public, equivalent to recognition and approval of his work, something always sought in each and every one of the bullfighting *suertes* from beginning to end. The other goal is to receive and slow down the bull in order to be able to *lidiar* it. This function, which is not always aesthetic, is, nevertheless,

important, because, above all else, the *suertes* are the answers which the torero must give to the problems raised by the bull in the course of its *lidia.* Therefore, bullfighting should be understood as a dialogue without words between the *toro* and the *torero*, a conversation in which the animal's needs and demands are presented, needs and demands which depend upon the bull's general characteristics, whether it charges clearly or reluctantly, whether it hooks with one horn or the other, or whether it has a short charge and is out to catch the matador... In that same conversation, the intelligence, bravery and skill of the torero will also come into play, and he will have to know how to make wise use of the different *suertes* at his disposal, in order to respond to the problems presented by the animal. Thus, if it is a strong charging bull, the matador will most likely decide to *doblarse* in the beginning, lowering his hands and giving tight passes, in order to force the bull to incline its head, thus reducing some of its strength. However, if the animal is a weaker one, then the matador would probably decide to execute *lances* with his feet together and hands held high, trying as much as possible to avoid obliging it to lower its head, and thus drain even more of its strength and power.

The aficionado who is capable, during the course of the *lidia*, of comprehending the language making up this dialogue — consisting of responses and counter-responses —, and who understands why the torero does what he does at each particular moment, or is able to realise when the professional is about to make a major mistake, doing just the opposite of what he should be doing, that spectator will derive far more pleasure and enjoyment out of the corrida. No serious aficionado contemplates the blood, the presence of which is indeed inevitable, nor does he revel in the bull's suffering, which is always regrettable, rather the sights of the experienced spectator focus merely on trying to understand the questions posed and the answers given by the different actors in this drama called *toreo*, which is being unfolded on the golden sands of the bullring. Therein lies the true and ultimate meaning of *Toreo,* along with that of knowing how to appreciate when a smooth, although complex movement of the arms, is creating a truly great *verónica* or merely a mediocre one, just one more of the general conglomerate of passes which have not and will not make history, nor be the least bit memorable.

VERÓNICA. JUAN MORA. "LA CAPRICHOSA". TALAVERA DE LA REINA (TOLEDO). 22-9-1991

KNEELING VERÓNICA. VÍCTOR PUERTO. "LAS VENTAS". MADRID. 7-10-2000

KNEELING VERÓNICA. JOSELITO. "LA TERCERA". SAN SEBASTIÁN DE LOS REYES (MADRID). 2-9-1994 >

CAPE LANCE OR PASS WITH FEET TOGETHER. ORTEGA CANO. "LAS VENTAS", MADRID. 24-10-1992

CAPE PASS OR LANCE WITH FEET TOGETHER. JOSELITO. "LAS VENTAS", MADRID. 28-5-1992 >

DELANTAL OR APRON PASS. EL JULI. "LAS VENTAS", MADRID, 15-6-2000

DELANTAL OR APRON PASS. JAVIER VÁZQUEZ. "LAS VENTAS", MADRID, 30-9-1993 >

All of the different *suertes* making up the complex art of bullfighting, *verónicas* and *lances*, whether they be good, bad or indifferent, should be *rematadas* or finished off. This is the finishing touch, the cherry on the top and very often the culminating moment of that particular facet of the *lidia*. And the *remate* pass is so important that the different variations with the cape can, in and of themselves, ruin a fine series of *verónicas*, or, to the contrary, make spectators forget that the set of *lances* they had just seen were only poor to middling. The *remates* can be either high or low passes (depending upon the strength of the bull), they can be graceful or austere (according to the torero's personality), profound or extravagant, extremely daring or more aesthetic; these aspects are irrelevant for all the aficionado really asks is that they be executed, with *torería*, purity and a great deal of truth.

The *remates* with the *capote* are like a wild card and consist of a group of twenty or more different *suertes*, each with a very distinct concept and purpose, which can be executed to end off even a single *verónica*. However, the day to day reality of today's *toreo* reveals that only a few *remates* are used with relative frequency. In fact, the half dozen most commonly repeated ones represent only a small percentage of the full range of possibilities at the *lidiador's* disposal.

The most important of all of them, first, because of its historical background, and second, because of its very concept and veracity, is the so-called *media verónica*, which as we will see later on, also admits a variety of interpretations. The *media verónica* can be executed on either horn and it is really an offshoot of the *verónica*, for to initiate the pass, the bullfighter offers the cape to the bull in the very same way, with the technical difference that instead of extending it palm-side forward, he presents the backs of his hands. Then, he leads the bull along, *toreado* and engaged in the cloth, until he bends gracefully at the waist and pulls the cape in at his right hip (if he is leading with his right hand and directing the pass at the animal's right horn). This *media verónica* is called a *belmontina* after Juan Belmonte (a revolutionary bullfighting figure during the first decades of the 20th century), who was a true master of its execution. The torero's feet should be separated, thus impressing upon the maneuver, not only a great deal of beauty, but also exceptional depth and purity. In this

media verónica, the bull is forced to restrain or slow down its charge, although this is not done in a brusque manner, but by making sure that the animal is fully engaged and submitted to the matador's cape. The *diestro* will usually conclude a *media verónica* by bringing his hands together, thus creating a great swirl and spread of the cape.

In addition to this *media verónica* executed with an open stance, feet widespread, there is another variation, which is performed *pies juntos* or feet together, which can be executed by standing directly in front of the animal or in a profile to its charge. This form of *media* proves to be less profound, although if done well, it is as aesthetic as the previous one, due to the fact the torero's figure is less stiff, more relaxed, and much more in control of the tempo of the bull and of the *toreo*. In this *media* pass, with the feet placed more or less together (depending upon the personal interpretation of each torero), the matador feels that he can exercise a great deal of control over the bull; that he, with his verticality, is like a pillar or post stuck in the middle of the sand, which obliges the animal to stop in the precise place and at the precise moment that he determines with a mere flick of the cape. It is, in reality, a question of desire and control: to leave the bull in the exact spot chosen by the torero and most probably against the animal's own will.

Logic seems to imply that the *verónicas* with feet apart should be followed by a *media* finishing pass performed with feet apart, and that the *lances* with the feet together, would call for a *media* with feet together; and this is frequently but not always the case... There is no obligation to proceed in this manner. Like everything in bullfighting, the *remates* are also totally subject to the inspiration of the moment, and to the fact that the bullfighter resorts to whatever he feels is going to prove most attractive to the spectators, because it is what the bull will most easily admit at that particular moment in its *lidia*.

Obviously, the *media verónicas* also have a kneeling version, with either one or both knees on the ground, which is executed with relative frequency and which adds an extra added touch of danger to its more classic form. It is quite common for a series of *verónicas* to be concluded with a *media de rodillas* or kneeling *media verónica*, in an attempt on the part of the torero to gain the public's favour with a dramatic maneuver

which allows no room for error, due to its difficult and dangerous execution, with his knees fixed firmly in the sand. It is indeed rare that after having given a kneeling *media*, the torero can add (link, is really the word), another one, for he has neither the time nor the physical space in which to turn about and offer the cape to the bull again.

The following group of more common *remates* we will cover now is that which is effected by releasing the cape with one hand and *toreando* only with the other. These are *suertes* which are very similar to the *naturales* and *derechazos* performed with the *muleta*, as we will see later on. These *lances* fall, then, within the category of *largas* although not all of them are referred to as such. The most common of all is the *revolera*, which takes its name from the ruffle of a full, flare skirt, for in its execution, the torero makes the cape open up and swirl around his waist. It is, of course, a very showy, spectacular *suerte* and one of enormous beauty if executed well, due to the way the cape is made to flow, while the torero passes it from one hand to the other behind his back, thus adding a special measure of colour and *alegría* to its execution. However, it is highly important to stress the fact that the *revolera* must be performed slowly with the matador wrapping himself up entirely in the cape and in the bull, at the same time that he spins around on his toes; if it is not performed in this manner and all the matador does is displace the animal with a brusque movement of the cape, the end result will not be very aesthetic. Far too often, there is only a very thin line between a well-done execution and a superficial one, lacking in truth and depth. Similar in their form, here in Bullfighting, more than anywhere else, appearances can really be deceiving.

Together with the *revoleras*, are the very common *remates* or finishing passes known as the *largas* (the normal *larga*, the *cordobesa*, the *afarolada* — in which the cape is passed over the head —, the *serpentina*, the *caracolina*...); all of these suggestive, provocative adornments require highly synchronised movements. They also feature a considerable amount of truth, for even though the cape unfolds in its entirety, the torero uses very little cloth to attract and *torear* the bull. From this point of view, it is highly important to advance the cape, in order to engage the animal at a distance and at just the right moment — and bring it along, immersed in the

cloth —, without any hesitation or sudden movements, which can provoke an unexpected reaction in the bull. In the *normal larga,* the cloth (that part of the cape which does the actual *toreo*) must be drawn out from below the horns with smooth control, marking the exit for the animal to follow, with a gentle movement of the wrist. The most complicated moment in the execution of the *larga* is when one hand releases the cloth and the other begins to *torear;* this should be done when the bull is neither too far away, nor too close, for in both cases, the torero would encounter serious problems of synchronisation. Except for the *largas cambiadas a porta gayola* (performed directly before the *toril* gates) or in the *tercio*, these are quite difficult to execute if the bull has not been entirely submitted and controlled beforehand. In other words, if the man has not managed to dominate the bull.

Another variation of the *larga* is the so-called *cordobesa* or *lagartijera*, named after Rafael Molina "Lagartijo", a great 19th century torero, born in Córdoba, who impressed so much personality on its execution that the *suerte* ended up bearing his name. In the *larga cordobesa*, after having followed all the steps involved in the normal *larga*, the torero must bring his hand up to his shoulder, allowing the cape to rest there and thus fall inertly all along his back. In this *larga*, just as important as the execution itself and the *toreo* of the bull, is the slow, majestic way in which the torero retreats from the animal, without looking back. He who manages to do this, not only leaves the bull fixed in its place, and mesmerized by how the bullfighter has managed to deceive it with his *toreo*, but also transmits to the public the matador's typical air of haughty self-satisfaction and arrogance. A distinction must be made if just one hand is used, for then the finishing pass would be called a *brionesa*, in which the cape is gathered up and swept over the bull's head.

At this point in the *lidia*, we have concluded the discussion on the receiving passes and their corresponding *remates*. The bull, which first burst into the ring with great strength and power, has now been slowed down considerably, for it has been fought with a three-fold purpose: first, to stop it from running aimlessly around the ring; and second, "to teach it" to charge, convincing it with human arguments — *temple* and smoothness — that it, too, can participate in the "fiesta" of the bullfight. "Teaching it to charge", means eliminating

all of its bad habits and *querencias* (homing instincts and tendencies to retreat to a particular place in the ring), if it evidenced such negative inclinations when it first charged out of the *chiqueros*, and it also means helping it, through the bullfighter's mastery, control and self-assurance, to develop its natural conditions for the *lidia*, innate in its brave blood, but which have never up until this moment had the opportunity to be put to the test.

The third and last of the goals of the receiving *suertes* seeks to reveal the bullfighter's artistic style, although certainly the two previous considerations should also be carried out in an aesthetic and harmonious manner, precisely because the final goal of all *toreo*, in addition to the *lidia* of the bull and the subsequent victory of man's intelligence over the animal's brute force, is clearly an artistic one. In reality, all of *toreo* is meant to be a continuous struggle between the substance and the form. Substance is, for example, the execution of the right techniques and maneuvers, which the animal requires at each moment in its *lidia* (the *toque* or flick of the cape, the distance, the height or level at which the cloths are handled, the torero's placement...), and they are always directed at obtaining the most brilliant results in the *faena*. Form, on the other hand, is made up of the different bullfighting *suertes* and the aesthetic way in which the techniques of the substance are put into practice. However, true *toreo*, that which becomes historical, immortal and leaves an indelible mark on aficionados, is the one which combines the substance and the form perfectly, and in such a fluid and natural manner that it proves to be almost imperceptible. There are, and always have been, great toreros of substance only, who have earned the respect and recognition of serious aficionados, and there are, and always have been great toreros of form, who were also readily accepted by the publics. However, there have not been nor are there today that many toreros who have been able to combine substance and form together, in order to attain the status of truly legendary figures of *Toreo*. They are called the "epoch-making" toreros, because their presence has overwhelmed and given true meaning to an entire era of bullfighting.

We should also mention the so-called effective aesthetics, that which the great *banderilleros* have employed when they fight a bull, seeking to put into practice the two main objectives explained above: stopping the animal from racing around the ring and, above all, teaching it to charge.

KNEELING HALF OR MEDIA VERÓNICA. ORTEGA CANO. "LAS VENTAS". MADRID. 25-5-1992

REVOLERA. CÉSAR RINCÓN. "LAS VENTAS". MADRID. 1-10-1991 >

REVOLERA. ENRIQUE PONCE. SEGOVIA. 30-6-1993

REVOLERA. FRASCUELO. "LAS VENTAS". MADRID. 12-10-1991 >

LARGA OR LONG PASS. JOSÉ TOMÁS. "LAS VENTAS". MADRID. 15-5-1998

LARGA OR LONG PASS. MANOLO CARRIÓN. VALENCIA. 22-7-1993 >

BRIONESA. CÉSAR RINCÓN. "LAS VENTAS", MADRID. 1-6-1992

LARGA CORDOBESA OR LONG PASS. ENRIQUE PONCE. "VISTA ALEGRE", BILBAO. 7-6-1992 >

Once the *lidia* has progressed to this point, what should follow is deep, pure *toreo*, the profound interpretation of the art and the most brilliant culmination of the matador's entire performance. With a little luck, the spectator has already seen this in the *verónicas* and in the receiving passes, and also in the *remates* or finishing passes executed either in a high or a low manner, but above all else with *torería* and elegance. And now this profound artistic interpretation should continue to prevail, following the bull's encounter with the picador and between each one of the *varas* or pics. The picing phase is undeniably a form of punishment, aimed at moulding and breaking in the animal for the *muleta*, the most fundamental part of Modern Tauromachy, which demands greater duration and performance, both from the bull as well as from the bullfighter. The picing or *suerte* de varas is vital because all of the *muleta* passes are given at a slower rate of movement than those of the cape — the so-called *temple* or tempering of the animal's charge —, and in order to do this, it is absolutely necessary to reduce the animal's strength, so that the torero can in turn impose his own tempo on his *toreo*. *Temple*, as we will see later on, is a magical concept, around which the fundamental *toreo* work, that which is done with the *muleta*, will revolve. However, there is still a lot more to see before the *faena,* because the horses are still in the ring. Unfortunately, they are clearly too ponderous and out of proportion for the strength and power of today's bull.

Between one pic and the next, or at the end of the first and only *vara* (which is regrettably, all spectators are likely to see nowadays), it becomes time for the *quites* or the artistic interventions with the cape. They are called *quites* from the word *quitar*, because this was its original purpose: to "remove" or separate the bull from the horse and finish off the action with a functional "*quite*", a graceful but rapid maneuver with the cape. However, throughout the evolution of *toreo*, the *lances* intended to remove the bull from the horse have gained in importance and have come to acquire their full and definitive significance thanks to both Spanish and Mexican bullfighters, who were, by tradition, highly inclined to invent and participate with fanciful creativity in this aspect of the *lidia*. And so, little by little, those *lances* which at the beginning had no purpose other than that of functional *lidia* (that which

corresponded merely to the "substance", as such), began to take on greater and greater significance, until we arrive at today's *tercio* or session of *quites*, which features an extensive variety of *suertes*, aimed solely and exclusively at the torero's artistic success. In addition, this is the only moment in the *lidia* in which the other matadors have the right to intervene and do some cape work with a colleague's bull. And a "right" it is indeed, because the matador to whom the animal being fought corresponds, cannot refuse to let another torero step in with the *capote* on his bull and "show off", perhaps even more than he himself had been able to do with this animal. If the matadors are also *banderilleros*, they might choose to place the *banderillas* themselves, in spectacular and daring displays, although in this particular *tercio* or aspect of the corrida, they have to first be invited to do so by the torero to whom the bull corresponds and can never undertake such a step on their own initiative.

In fact, the true and underlying *raison d'être* of the *quites*, lied precisely in the creation of a wonderful competitive display and artistic rivalry between the respective matadors, in order to see who could best entertain the public. Nevertheless, the reality is indeed much more prosaic: the bulls almost never receive the three prescribed *puyazos*, and many do not even receive two, a circumstance which prevents the other bullfighters on the bill from competing with the matador whose bull it is, in the *tercio de quites*. It is a great misfortune for bullfighting and for the spectacle itself that on far too many occasions, the *quites* have been reduced to a mere and insignificant formality, which tiptoes along, between the initial cape passes and the *muleta* work.

Nevertheless, there is, certainly, a truly immense variety of cape *quites*, and options open to any torero who wishes to enter into full competition with his colleagues. What we are most likely to see nowadays is that this aspect of the corrida is reduced to the intervention of just two matadors: the actual matador, whose bull it is, and the one whose name appears next on the programme.

As we well know, a *quite* refers to the group of *lances* executed with the cape, between one *puyazo* and the next, or, more extensively, those *suertes* which the torero uses to remove or position

the bull before the picador's horse. By pure methodological distinction, and in addition to the evident differences in their execution, we can divide the *quites* into two fundamental groups: those which are effected by the matador with the cape held in front of him; and those which he performs with the cape behind his back. However, we should clarify the fact that despite such marked differences in execution, the final goal within the context of the *lidia* is basically the same: the pursuit of artistic success. Also important to take into account is the honest, but heated rivalry between the toreros, their desire to participate and excel, to be more daring or more artistic, or simply more *torero* than their colleagues. The audience, with their enthusiastic applause, will be the impartial judges who issue the verdict as to who has won this little duel between matadors. Furthermore, there is no doubt that a good *quite* predisposes the spectators favorably for the oncoming *faena* with the *muleta*, but it is also true that a fine *quite* executed by a colleague (who proves to be far braver or more skilled than the one whose bull it is) can only serve to show up the matador who must fight and kill that particular animal afterwards. Obviously the matador whose turn it is always has the last word and he can "patch" things up with the *muleta*; although it is also evident that the torero who is capable of revealing his true valour, skill, art and worth at this early point in the corrida to the public's full satisfaction, has progressed that much closer to his final goal of success and professional recognition.

The most common *quite* performed with the cape held in front of the torero's body is — in addition to the *verónica* — the *chicuelina*, which takes its name from Sevillian matador Manuel Jiménez "Chicuelo", a torero of enormous importance in the evolution of bullfighting, and who practised his art between 1920 and 1950. "Chicuelo" was also a fine *lidiador* who enjoyed considerable popularity in Mexico and served to bridge the gap between both tauromachies. The *chicuelina* is a *suerte* in which the torero faces and cites the bull, and as it charges, he wraps himself up in the cape, spinning around simultaneously on his toes in order to be perfectly re-positioned and ready to repeat the *lance*, with the *capote* spread out and extended in front of him. The most important part of this

suerte, of course, is the placement, height and positioning of the hands, which will be what distinguishes a graceful *chicuelina* from a clumsier one. "Chicuelo" claimed that in order to perform this *lance* correctly, the hands had to be held high, in a position similar to that adopted for dancing *sevillanas* or flamenco. It was an obvious simile, which in reality reflected the underlying aspect of elegance and graceful movement, found in both the dance and the execution of the *chicuelina*. According to the Sevilla-born matador, in the *suerte* which bears his name, the hands had to be raised more or less to shoulder level, with the one marking the path the bull is to follow, held slightly higher (in other words: the right hand, if one is executing the *chicuelina* on the bull's right flank). This is the hand which actually does the *toreo,* a point which embodies one of the main characteristics being repeated continuously in all cape work in which the cloth is held in both hands: despite the fact that both intervene, only one hand really *torea*, and the other one just goes along and accompanies it. *Torear* obviously means *poder* (domination), *engañar* (deception) and *burlar* (trickery and illusion); therefore, one hand sets the rhythm and speed, cites and collects the bull and marks the path and tempo, it will follow, while the other supports and accompanies the lead hand, the one with the power, patiently awaiting its turn, which will come when the *lance* is repeated on the bull's other horn, at which point the roles are cleanly inverted. It might so happen that there are toreros who are far more skilled with one hand than with the other (generally but not necessarily the one they write with) and their performance on one horn might prove more elegant than on the other.

It is important to make a distinction between a *quite* as such and the execution of any of these *suertes* in an isolated manner (for example, a *chicuelina* can be used as the *remate* for a series of receiving *verónicas*), but it is the torero's desire to link up a series of similar *lances* one after the other, which makes up a *quite*. One *chicuelina*, no matter how splendid it may be, does not a *quite* make, and the linking together of three or four, on both horns, manifests the torero's ability to continually re-position himself correctly and relate to the bull. Furthermore, only the linking of several *lances* at just the right

moment, will enable the matador to elicit the right response from the public. This is the only way to reach and "move" the spectators.

The *chicuelina* admits, like all *toreo*, interpretations, according to each matador's personal way of thinking or feeling. And if the one executed by "Chicuelo" was done with the his hands held high (an interpretation adopted years later by Paco Camino, another great torero, active in the rings between the 1960s and 1980s), José María "Manzanares" (1970s to 1990s) chose to perform this same *lance* by lowering his hands considerably, especially the dominant one, which he would sometimes drop to knee level. This *chicuelina*, executed with such great artistry and impact, is aesthetically different, although identical in regard to the essential movements which the matador must follow.

There is certainly another fundamental aspect which differentiates one interpretation from the other: the bull with which it can be executed. It is highly unlikely that "Manzanares" could perform this kind of *chicuelina* with a weak, lame animal, because when he forces it to lower its head, the animal would probably end up falling down. This brings us to yet another significant consideration in the *quites*: that in addition to their being adorning *suertes*, they also carry out a substantial function during the *lidia*. The *quite* which the matador chooses to perform should be in accord with the conditions of the bull: low hands for a strong bull, high hands for a weak one, stillness for a good charging animal, and movement for one with little mobility. That is, the *quites* employed in this *tercio* should once again be considered artistic recourses in relation with the technical problems raised by the bulls.

The silent dialogue we have already seen assumes its full importance anew, because the best torero is not the one who is the bravest or most daring, but he who is not only brave and daring, but more intelligent when deciding on how best to interpret the needs of each animal and, thus, provide the most appropriate responses. Attempting to go against the logic established in this dialogue usually leads to failure, the majority of the time. In this sense, the *quites* in which the torero raises his hands the highest are the *tafalleras* and the *faroles*, which as we will see later on, are magnificent artistic recourses for

weak bulls. Those which involve the most movement (on the part of the matador) are the *navarras*, making them highly suitable for short-charging bulls. We wish to remind our readers that *toreo* is, in the end, a continuous selection of *suertes* (and, by extension, a rejection of others), those which the torero feels to be most appropriate at each moment. This implies, of course, that the *lidiador* can be right or wrong, both in the approach and development of his *faena*, as well as in the selection of the *suertes* which give it form; thus a correct or incorrect choice can lead ultimately, either to success or failure.

Another variation of the *chicuelina* is what is called in Spain the *al paso* or walking *lance*, and, in Mexico, the *quite por las afueras*, created by the great Mexican torero Pepe Ortiz, an undisputed master of *toreo* with the cape — he handled the *capote* with unrivalled creativity and imagination —, and his name will be repeated over and over again in the course of this text. The fundamental difference between the *chicuelina al paso* and the *quites por las afueras* does not lie in the execution, which is identical, but in their moment of execution. *Chicuelinas al paso* are given when the torero decides to walk the bull to the horse; the *quites por las afueras* is performed in the same manner, but to remove the bull from the picador. Thus, in the former, the *lidiador* proceeds from the centre of the ring to the area known as the *tablas*, near the fence; and in the second, he goes from the "inside" terrains near the fence, towards the centre of the ring, called the "*afueras*", or exteriors. There are no other differences, although this distinction in and of itself is sufficient for both *suertes* to merit their own, separate names.

Before moving on and leaving behind the *suerte* to which "Chicuelo" lent his name, there are several other important aspects which should be mentioned in relation with the *chicuelina*, a *lance* which, in this sense, is rather paradigmatic. The first question is that of the names given to the different bullfighting maneuvers. We know that this *suerte* is called the "*chicuelina*", after Manuel Jiménez. Sometimes, as is the case here, the torero who has "patented" the pass, so to speak, was also its inventor (even though there is another version which has been attributed to "Llapisera", a comic bullfighter who performed this *suerte* or a highly similar one with comic overtones). However, it might also happen that the *suerte* was really invented

by another torero, or by no-one in particular, or it merely formed a part of the long-standing collection of traditional passes, and yet, due to the personal and magnificent interpretation of one specific matador, that *suerte* was awarded his name. No-one had ever really queried or challenged these honourific appellations because, by that time, the torero in question has already become sufficiently respected and famous.

The names of the *suertes* can also be variations, either diminutive or augmentative, of the matador or of the city or bullring in which they were performed for the very first time. It might occur that a pass has a recognized author, but that another torero has made it famous, and so it acquires the name of the latter bullfighter, much to the displeasure of the first. It can also be the case that two matadors dispute the invention and authorship of a particular *suerte*, sometimes due to one's lack of knowledge about the other's contribution, and at other times, due to obvious creative and professional vanities.

However, what seems to occur most often and no-one really knows why, is that the matadors who are recognized as the authors of a particular *suerte* tend to deny their authorship. They all customarily claim that the particular pass emerged quite by accident, while they were trying to execute an entirely different one. It is as if they are afraid of being credited with inventing something new and prefer to protect themselves by saying that it happened by chance or... by magic. As a result, "Chicuelo" insisted that he had performed his very first *chicuelina*, in Valencia in 1920, without really having given it much thought. He added that, despite all the commotion it caused, when he reached the hotel, he had completely forgotten what he had done, and that only when he stood in front of the mirror, beside his trusted *banderillero*, was he able to re-create one of the *suertes,* which, over the years, has acquired so much popularity. We do not want to contradict "Chicuelo", nor do we doubt the veracity of his explanation, but that is the same story which many other toreros have told before and after him. Perhaps we have to believe in the influence of the "good fairies" in the creation of the bullfighting *suertes*; although we are also more inclined to think that the toreros are, for some reason, reluctant to admit they are the creators of a *suerte* which may initially stray from the basic canons of Classicism.

A *suerte* frequently performed is the *navarra*, a direct descendant of the oldest, most classic *toreo*, which was already catalogued in the very first texts written or inspired by toreros, such as "Pepe-Hillo" and "Paquiro", in the 18th and 19th centuries. Navarrese-style bullfighting in its origins always concluded with movement, even though the torero began by standing perfectly still, in order to prove his determination and bravery in the face of his adversary. Navarrese *toreo* was just that: firm and still in the beginning, and light and mobile at the end. The *navarra* pass exemplifies this concept very well, for in the beginning, the *suerte* came into being as a *delantal* or "apron pass", performed with the feet together. The bull is engaged in the cloth and when its horns have passed the torero's body, the matador begins to spin on his heels and gracefully walks away, in order to seek the right distance at which to repeat the *suerte*. His arms should be outspread and separated from his body so that the cape can be extended in its entirety, resembling wings which swirl about in time with the bullfighter's movement, in order to accompany the bull's charge. The true elegance of the *navarra* lies in the matador having the sufficient serenity so as to turn slowly and smoothly, with no brusqueness, nor clumsiness, because the moment in which he loses sight of the bull (when he begins to turn and the animal is left behind him) is a very difficult one; he never really knows — although he can guess — just how much distance lies between him and the animal. Therefore, even though it is a moving *suerte*, and the main virtue of *toreo* lies in its stillness, the perfect execution of the *navarra* is not without its merit, and it is one of the *suertes*, together with the *chicuelina*, which is executed most often at present.

It so happens that "Chicuelo" is also associated indirectly with the creation of this *suerte*, although perhaps only in regard to its Mexican name, for when the Sevilla-born torero went to Mexico and performed a *quite* of *navarras*, the spectators who were not at all familiar with it, automatically dubbed it the "*chicuelina*". Then, when he performed the real *chicuelina* years later, the *navarra* was renamed the *chicuelina antigua* (old *chicuelina*), in order to differentiate it from the "modern" one, they had just seen. And that name persists even today, in memory of a torero of a past epoch, although it was made clear a long time ago that the *navarra* was neither a *suerte* created by "Chicuelo", nor is there any reason for it to bear his name.

We have already mentioned in passing two new *suertes* or *quites* with the cape held in front of the torero's body: the *farol* and the *tafallera*. A great deal has been recorded about this latter *suerte* in the annals of Tauromachy, between Spain and Mexico, where it has been known by a variety of other names. Another Sevilla-born matador, Luis Muñoz Hoyo "Marchenero" first created it in Spain (and there are references to one of his appearances in Madrid in 1915, in which he included this *suerte* in his performance), although when he went to Mexico later on, he performed it there frequently and with relative success. Nicanor Villalta (Cretas, Teruel, 1897 – Madrid, 1980) must have seen him execute it in South America and Villalta made it so popular, that it eventually took on his name. First, it was called the *villaltina*, and later, the *tafallera*, for it is said that it was performed for the first time in public, in the Navarra town of Tafalla. Whatever the case, the *tafallera (villaltina* or *marchenera)*, is an unstressful *quite* of alleviation for the bulls, due to the fact that it is performed by raising both arms as the bull lowers its head to charge. Then, the cape is allowed to slide all along the bull's back, sweeping along with the utmost smoothness. The fact that it can be performed with feet together or apart, does not furnish it with greater or lesser merit, nor is it given a different name. Another, kneeling version is also possible, which is of far greater risk, due to the considerable difficulty experienced by the torero when he raises both hands above his head, while crouching on his knees.

The entire group of *quites* called *faroles* feature one common characteristic: the torero must raise both arms (and, consequently, the cape) over his head. It is a fine way to end a *suerte*, for the bull has already been *toreado* and deceived an instant before, when his hands were held at the animal's eye level. There are two different ways to execute this *suerte*: the normal *farol* and the *invertido or inverted farol.* In the first one, the torero cites the bull with his chest and without moving his feet, he marks the path for the animal to follow by raising his hands above his head; in the second version, the *diestro* inverts the position of his body, receiving the bull from behind, after having made a perfect 180° turn in the precise moment that the animal reaches the correct distance — which is called the torero's jurisdiction —.

The resolution of the *suerte* is the same: once he is situated with his back to the bull, the matador raises his arms above his head and in this way marks the path for the bull to continue.

There are two *suertes* found mid-way between the *quites* with the cape gathered in front of the torero's body and those which are held behind him: the *medio* or half *farol* and the *caleserina*. We can call them bridge or connecting *suertes*, because they serve, before a moving bull, to bring the cape from one side of the matador's body to the other. With the *medio farol*, the *diestro* embarks the bull from in front of his body, raises the cape above his head, and ends up with the cloth behind his back, opening the way to a variety of different *suertes* with the cape held behind him. In the *caleserina*, the torero embarks the bull with the cape clutched behind him, and with a turn of his body, his right arm passes the cape over his head again, leaving it directly in front of his body, so that he can continue with the execution of an entirely different *suerte*, perhaps a *revolera* or a *larga*, depending upon his fancy and inspiration at that particular moment. It should be kept in mind at all times that *toreo* — what we see in the arena — is influenced, on the immense majority of the occasions, by the torero's own creativity and spontaneous artistic inspiration. The torero must be able to furnish immediate solutions to the bull's specific needs at any one moment in the course of the *lidia*. We may commonly see a *quite* in which a half *farol* and a *caleserina* are combined, creating an arrangement of two very differing elements, which cannot as yet boast their own name.

As regards the *suertes* executed with the cape behind the torero's back, the undisputed leader is the *gaonera*, a *suerte* which together with the *verónica* and the *natural* make up what can be termed the trilogy of the most fundamental *suertes* in *Toreo*, each one executed at a different moment in the *lidia* of the bull. The *gaonera* possesses all the truth of the *verónica* (because it is, in reality, a *verónica* with the cape held behind the back) and of the *natural* (because it is really a *natural*, performed with the cape). However, the *gaonera* also features an additional and important complication: due to the fact that the torero moves his arms behind his body, the movements are quite limited, as is the scope of the

charge which he can impose upon the bull. The *gaonera* has always represented a kind of challenge, a challenge which the torero performing the *quite*, throws out at his colleagues like a gauntlet, in order to see who will accept the call to a duel.

The *quite* of *gaoneras* executed by Madrid matador José Tomás in the San Isidro Fair of Madrid, in 1999, was the most colossal moment seen up until that moment in the entire Fair. On a very windy afternoon, José Tomás adopted a stance at a considerable distance from the bull and with incredible smoothness and staging, swung the cape behind his back, which began to flap about like a flag on a pole. He impressed upon his movements so much sense of ritual and temperance, that even before the bull had begun to charge, José Tomás had already won over the public and at the same time got the better of his colleagues. Such was his display of bravery and raw courage, even before he had performed that very first *gaonera*, that he was immediately able to captivate the spectators with his incredible show of self-confidence and the profound truth of his *toreo*. And it could be said that another gale wind began to bluster through the Madrid bullring, even greater than the one already blowing; it was like a wonderful hurricane of stirring excitement and thrilling elation. In that precise instant, even before he had begun to *torear*, it was evident that an unforgettable expression of *toreo* was going to take place in the Las Ventas arena, in the most absolute and fullest sense of the word. The bull broke into a charge, and a sudden gust of real wind, which had nothing to do with the spiritual one, disarmed the torero, who was knocked down by the bull, fortunately without sustaining any serious injury. Back on his feet, he recovered his cape and tossed it behind his back, but this time he resolved the *quite* with a series of magnificent *gaoneras*, so extraordinary in their difficulty, that by the end of the *suerte*, José Tomás had emerged as the absolute *triunfador* (star) of the entire Fair and people would not stop talking about him. Then, he proceeded to re-confirm everything he had already achieved, with the *muleta*, but that is yet another story, which we will not go into here.

The *gaonera* was created by Mexican maestro Rodolfo Gaona, an outstanding bullfighting figure between 1908 and 1924, who reinterpreted in his very own fashion the old bullfighting maneuver called *De frente por detrás,* a series of four different *suertes* all linked together, of which only the third was really similar to what we call the *gaonera* today. Other *quites* which might be performed with the *capote* behind the matador's back, are the *mariposa* (Butterfly), created by Spaniard Marcial Lalanda; the *tapatía*, the *orticina*, the *rogerina* and the *quites de oro*, all four, invented by Pepe Ortiz; the s*altillera*, of Fermín Espinosa "Armillita" (similar to the *gaonera*, with the only difference that it is executed solely on the right side and the hand holding the cape is raised above the bull); the *talaverana*, of "Morenito de Talavera"; the *fregolina*, of Romero Freg; the *vizcaína*, of Arturo Alvarez "El Vizcaíno"; and, among many others, the *crinolina*, of Eliseo Gómez "El Charro". Almost all of the foregoing matadors were of Mexican origin.

As always, the *gaonera* admits a more daring, kneeling version, which was executed frequently by "Armillita". In all of these *suertes*, what stands out above all other considerations is the desire to please the spectators and display one's courage and determination; in other words, putting one's life on the line in order to triumph, by willingly assuming all the difficulties involved in the execution, in the hope of impressing a spirit and *alegría* on the *tercio de quites*. As we have already said, these *suertes* are like the "gauntlet", which the torero throws down before his colleagues in order to challenge and defeat them in clean and honourable competition and convince the general public that he is not only the best, but also the most noble, valiant and worthy heir to centuries of integrity, valor and *torería*. Such a torero is determined to delight the public with the truth of his *toreo*, at the same time that he deceives and dominates the bull and defies Death, with absolute poise, grace and elegance.

GAONERA. MARTÍN ANTEQUERA. "LAS VENTAS", MADRID. 30-5-2000

SALTILLERA. MIGUEL ABELLÁN. "LAS VENTAS", MADRID. 29-5-2000 >

A sudden sounding of the *clarín* or bugle signals the end of the *tercio de quites*, and the fact that the *lidia* is heading towards its most fundamental aspect, the *toreo de muleta*, the final *tercio* or act, in which the matadors must do their utmost to consummate their final triumph. Everything which has occurred up until now might have been valid and important, with a great deal of variety and technical and artistic content, but in general, it has all been directed at preparing the animal for the last act, the final ten minutes in which both the bull and the bullfighter must reveal their true qualities and identities. When the *faena* reaches this point, there is no room for excuses or regrets, and what the *diestro* does not manage to accomplish in this period of time, will never be. When this page is turned, there is no going back: there is no way to recover the time lost, wasted or squandered.

However, there is still one more preliminary step to be followed, which is also of utmost importance: the *tercio de banderillas* — also called the *avivadores* or "rousers" —. These sticks, decorated with brightly coloured paper, are intended to decongest the bull after its experience with the cumbersome horse, with which it has suffered a great deal of punishment. The *banderillas* really infer very little harm on the animal, for one of their goals is precisely the contrary: that of reviving it, making it break into a run, giving it new impetus and readying it for the final act, the *tercio* of the *muleta*. Everything which occurs during the *tercio de banderillas* takes on enormous importance, as the bull which has been changing, for better or for worse during the course of the *lidia*, at this precise moment, generally undergoes yet another, very often more drastic evolution, which should be carefully noted. For this reason, while the members of his *cuadrilla* or matador's team prepare the bull for the placing of the sticks (sometimes the matador decides to place them himself, in order to gain the public's favor), the *diestro* studies the evolutions experienced by the animal very closely, for the bull he fought with the *capote* might have shown radically different behavior to the one he must face with the *muleta*. It is for this same reason, too, that the matador values so highly the more skilled and accomplished *subalternos* or *banderilleros,* who are capable of teaching the bull to charge correctly, of not showing it bad habits, of polishing and eliminating its bad tendencies and *querencias*, and finally, of revealing to the matador what its true characteristics are.

DOBLÓN OR DOUBLING PASS. WITH ONE KNEE ON THE GROUND. MANOLO CARRIÓN. "LAS VENTAS". MADRID. 4-7-1993

Nothing of what is done in the *lidia* is superfluous or of vacuous content, much less these cape passes, which the *banderilleros* perform with two hands and never with one, during the *tercio de banderillas*. The matador, attentive to every detail, takes careful mental note, recording new behaviors and erasing old ones, and depending upon what he sees in the animal, that is how he will commence his *faena* with the *muleta*. The receiving *muletazos* or *muleta* passes, which are the first ones given to the bull with the smaller red cloth, have two major objectives, according to their purpose: they can be used for adornment or effectiveness, although most commonly it is through adornment that effectiveness is sought. Just as we saw with the cape, everything will depend upon the strength and the condition of the bull and no two animals exhibit the same behavior: if the animal is still very strong, even after the *tercio de varas*, the matador will most likely decide to "punish" it further with a *doblón* or tight turning, doubling pass, which attains its maximum expression of *torería* when performed in a kneeling fashion. In this *suerte*, the matador takes the *muleta* in one hand, either in the right and draped over the sword (which would then be called *ayudados* or aided passes), or in the left, and he makes the bull turn in tightly. However, it is not meant to be a punishment intended to finish off the bull, but rather its purpose is to reduce the strength the animal still possesses, so that it becomes suitable material for the most fundamental *toreo*, which will follow in due course.

It might so happen that the bull appears to conserve just the right amount of strength, but the matador will need to test it and determine the physical condition of the animal after its presumable transformation during the *tercio de banderillas*; in this case, he will definitely fight with the *muleta* held high. He will discover its true condition, without punishing it, by raising his hands and moving the cloth along carefully — assisting it, is the term —, in an effort to understand and accommodate himself to the animal, which he does not look upon as an enemy, but as a collaborator, who is going to help him achieve success. If these high passes or *suertes* are performed with the *muleta* held in both hands, as we have suggested above, and with the feet spread apart, they are called *ayudados por alto* or aided high passes. They are *estatuarios* or statuary passes, when the bullfighter, resembling a vertical, hieratic effigy, adopts a closed stance, feet

together, and does not move a single muscle of his body. There are many more utilitarian ways to begin the *faena*, such as, with the *pase de costadillo*, in which the torero holds the *muleta* in his right hand, cites the bull to charge with the cloth held high and just at the moment when the animal lowers its head into the cloth, the matador turns slightly, offering it his side (*costado*). It is important in the execution and conclusion of this *suerte*, for the torero to slide the *muleta* over the bull — sweeping it all along its back —, a movement which provides a sensation of *temple* and profound *torería*, as well as of tranquility and repose on the part of the torero.

However, the matador, spurred on by his desire to triumph, can also begin the *faena* with a series of more daring *suertes*, which go beyond mere effectiveness, in order to achieve an extreme and uncompromisingly dramatic display, aimed at winning over the public by creating a feeling of maximum tension and excitement. Of course, the greater the risk assumed by the torero, the more impressive these *suertes* will be. In fact, it is quite common to see the matador begin by imposing a brusque change on the bull's charge, in an effort to produce a stirring and striking commencement to the *faena*.

Within this group of thrilling *suertes* executed at the beginning of the *faena*, we can find the *pedresina*, performed either standing up or kneeling down, which was invented fifty years ago by Pedro Martínez "Pedrés". In this pass, the torero adopts a position facing the *barrera* and very close to it. He cites the bull to charge in the direction of the *tablas* or fence, in a terrain in which it is physically impossible for the animal to fit. When, after a long run, the bull enters the matador's jurisdiction, the torero turns sharply at the waist — but without changing his position —, and unfolds the *muleta* behind his back. Similar to the *pedresina* is another *muleta* pass bearing the unusual name of *cartucho de pescado* or "roll of fish", in which the torero faces the bull, cites it with the *muleta* gathered up and grasped in his hand, and he does not let it fall open until the animal is very close to his body. Mention should also be made of the *litrazo*, created by Miguel Báez "Litri", in which the torero hides the *muleta* behind his back with his right hand. However, in this pass, it cannot be rolled up, as it is mounted on the sword, which extends it and gives it form. All of these

suertes in which the bull's full run and the uncertainty of the final resolution are involved, make for very effective and flashy initiations of *faena*s, for they impress the spectators, with the very evident risk assumed by the matador.

That dramatic sensation of danger can be carried to its final extremes, when the *diestro* begins his *faena* on his knees, *toreando* with either high or low passes, normal passes or with *faroles* similar to those he executes with the cape. Or he can begin by sitting on the white, wooden *estribo* or step of the *barrera,* which protrudes from the fence and which the toreros use for leverage to boost themselves over the side into the *callejón,* in a moment of danger. More spectacular still is to begin the *faena* seated in a chair, or kneeling down on a church *prie dieu*, or even sitting on the ground.

Each successive *suerte* is a link in that chain which seeks "the most difficult feat yet" and is like a new rung on the ladder the torero must climb in order to gain the public's favour. He must charm them with his determination and courage, delight them with the execution of a *suerte* which breaks with the more classic canons and transmit his determination and *alegría* and total disregard for his physical integrity and well-being. Nothing is more unattractive than a sloppy execution of these *suertes*, clouded over by a feeling of "*I really want to, but I am afraid and can't*", or any unforgivable, last minute misgivings. On the other end of the scale is success and the public's worshipping of valor as the ultimate recourse of bullfighting. There is another even greater recourse which is that of Art, for which it is necessary to possess even greater valor, for nothing is more difficult than fighting slowly and well, as we explained when we discussed the *verónica*. And there is a great deal of art to be found in the execution of the *suertes* carried out with two hands — the so-called *ayudados* or aided passes —, and also in the most fundamental ones, the *naturales* (left-handed passes) and the *derechazos* (right-handed passes), and in their respective *remates*, usually *pases de pecho* or chest passes, which should feature the same *torería,* elegance and sentiment. Valor here is the sustenance of *toreo*, the invisible pillars which make it possible to *torear,* the true substance which gives full meaning to the form.

AYUDADO POR ALTO OR AIDED HIGH PASS. JAVIER VÁZQUEZ. "LAS VENTAS", MADRID. 31-5-1993

PEDRESINA. JAVIER VÁZQUEZ. "LAS VENTAS", MADRID. 31-5-1993 >

KNEELING FAROL. JAVIER VÁZQUEZ. "LAS VENTAS", MADRID. 29-6-1994

MULETAZO SEATED ON THE BARRERA STEP. JAVIER VÁZQUEZ. "LAS VENTAS", MADRID. 29-6-1994 >

Fundamental *toreo* is that whose execution is at present absolutely necessary in order for a *faena* to achieve the necessary category and content, and henceforth, be properly appreciated by the aficionados. It might so happen that due to the poor condition of the bull, it will not be possible to apply any of the fundamental *suertes* with the *muleta* in its *lidia*, but other recourses are also meritorious, especially when they are executed with valor and sincerity and a knowledgeable public will be able to value the matador's work appropriately. However, nowadays, due to the evolution of *toreo*, which is focussing more and more on aesthetic aspects, rather than on *lidiador* ones, it is not likely that a more functional rather than an artistic *lidia* will ever evoke equivalent enthusiasm in the audience. We will not go into the subject of the *toreo* of recourses — involving *suertes* based on the matador's continual movement and on superficial passes given from one horn to the other, or chopping passes in front of the animal's face —, which are only useful with bad bulls, for we prefer to concentrate on the more fundamental maneuvers, which give greater form, depth and content to the *toreo* with the *muleta;* those passes which offer the torero the true possibility to triumph. In this sense, it becomes clear that *toreo* has undergone a very drastic evolution, for although it is true that this unique art form came into being as a preparation of the bull for its death — all the *suertes* had that function and no other —, what takes priority over all else now is *toreo* itself; the idea of guiding the bull back and forth, with trickery and deception, and putting aside the reality of its almost inevitable death.

The most important of all the fundamental *suertes* is the *pase natural*, executed with the left hand, without any assistance from the sword, which will remain in the right, dangling parallel to the matador's right leg. This *suerte* is performed in a straight or semi-straight line and always in a regular direction, that is, the left hand citing the left horn. These *muleta*zos are linked to one another in a totally circular fashion, giving the *faena* a unified sense of tandems, which will usually be finished off with the high chest pass, executed by the same hand on the bull's opposite side. Only this should be considered a *natural*, for the *muleta*zo with the left hand on the bull's right flank (such as, the chest pass), is

considered "contrary *toreo*", in contrast with the *regular* pass. The *pase natural* admits a very infrequent version with the right hand, as long as the *muleta* is held without the sword. The pass executed with the right hand holding the *muleta* mounted on the sword — the *derechazo*, as important in a *faena* as the *natural* — cannot, from my point of view, be considered a *natural* (although it follows the regular line of the bull's charge). This is because the most prominent characteristic of the *natural* is that it is executed without the support of the sword, thus allowing the *muleta* to fall freely, limited only by its own span and without any external prolongations. In other words, there is a naturalness and grace in the fall of the cloth.

This idea of "naturalness" is not a banal matter in *toreo*, for what gives true merit to the execution of the passes is, among other considerations, the extension of the surface area of the *muleta* which is presented to the bull. However, the matter is not so simple, because many other factors intervene in that evaluation, such as the situation of the torero himself, or the closeness with which he passes the bull, or the risk he assumes in the execution of the *muleta*zo. The total or balance of all of these elements serves to enhance the value of a *faena*. In any event, there are passes which involve a greater intrinsic risk, and among them, the *natural* stands out, the unchallenged sovereign of *toreo* with the *muleta*, and, as we have seen, a worthy companion to the *verónica* and the *gaonera*.

The origin of the *natural* developed simultaneously with the very origins of *toreo*. It is highly likely that when a man used a cloth for the very first time, centuries ago — perhaps his own cape folded in half —, in order to deceive the charge of a bull, he executed the first *natural* in history. There is, then, no real author or inventor, even though there does exist a long list of toreros who have, over the years (more than two hundred, if we refer just to the written records), furnished a variety of solutions, which were like milestones lining the path along which the *natural* matured into the pass we can admire today. This bullfighting *suerte* has come a long way indeed, the sum total of all the brilliant inspiration of countless toreros, some known and some anonymous, throughout the very evolution of bullfighting itself.

In a very brief manner, we can establish the following evolutionary steps in the history of the *natural*: To its initial execution, performed one by one without any intention of connecting them to each other, Rafael Guerra "Guerrita" (1862-1941) supplied the theoretical sense of the linking of one *natural* to the next (even though he did not use that word, which is a more modern term). During the first two decades of the 20th century, two colossal toreros coincided in the rings, José Gómez "Gallito" and Juan Belmonte, who, together, established the foundation for modern-day *toreo*. This is neither the appropriate place nor the time to speak of the true magnitude of these two Sevilla-born matadors, and it will have to suffice to say that without this grandiose pair, who differed so much from one another in the ring but were such good friends outside of it, Bullfighting today would have neither rhyme nor reason. Among many other contributions, "Gallito" was the first to link the *natural* around his body, forcing the bull's charge into a fundamental semi-circle. Belmonte, who linked far fewer *muleta*zos, nevertheless, discovered man's ability to enter the dangerous terrain of the bull and impose his wishes over the animal's will. "*Torear* within the bull itself", is the taurine expression which reflects that discovery, which turned the bull's straight charge into a curved one. That is the so-called *toreo cruzado* or crossover bullfighting, which is absolutely basic and essential. Belmonte also attributed a great deal of importance to the *cite* or citing, the first stage of both the *natural* and the *derechazo*, in which the torero, very tightly situated between the eyes and horns of the bull, calls to it from a distance in order to engage its attention on the *muleta* from afar.

But if "Guerrita" theorised about linked *toreo*, "Chicuelo", who has already appeared frequently in this text or "journey" of ours through the basics of Bullfighting, is credited with the definitive linking of the passes. According to historian Néstor Luján, "Chicuelo" was the creator of the true rhythm of modern *toreo*, with the gentle and flowing linking of the *faenas*". And along with Manuel Jiménez, there was another "Manuel", Manuel Rodríguez "Manolete" (1917-1947), the tragic hero, who like "Gallito", died in a small town bullring, gored by a bull which killed him at the height of his youth and glory, while converting

him, at the same time, into an immortal legend and a part of the eternal history of *toreo*. "Manolete" assumed the legacy left to him by his predecessors, while he contributed to the history of *toreo*, with his own concept of a *faena* structured around a series of *muletazos* (*naturales* or *derechazos*), which would embody the culmination of all the ideas and past achievements of "Guerrita", "Gallito" and "Chicuelo", among countless other valiant toreros. "Manolete" dazzled the publics, who had never before seen the likes of his *toreo*: one *natural* following another, and another, and still another... And after the finishing pass or *remate,* another five passes, and once again five more, and all of them, linked together in the very same spot, until it was the bull who gave out in the end. So great was his influence that some toreros even today show a very clear "Manolete" influence, even though fifty years have transpired since his death in Linares (Jaén). After Manuel Rodríguez, contributions to *toreo* have been both aesthetic as well as technical, related to the movement of the wrist, the height of the cloth in the citings and the impressive way the bull's terrain is invaded, with heavy emphasis placed on the importance of harmony and beauty. This is the *pase natural* in the year 2000: the technical and aesthetic culmination of all the advancements, some of which were barely noticeable, while others appeared more drastic; evolution and revolution have prevailed over the last two hundred years.

We have already said that there is nothing more genuine than a *natural* pass, executed with absolute purity. And this must be true, for at no point in the *lidia* of a bull does the public feel so fascinated, seduced and impassioned, as when a series of perfect *naturales* are being executed in a bullfight, with greater or lesser complications depending upon the conditions of the animal and even the weather. In fact, wind and rain are indeed the worst companions of *toreo*, two elements which only serve to drown or confuse it. And perhaps for this very reason, Madrid's Las Ventas plaza is so important, because not only does it offer very impressive animals to a very demanding public, but it is also a ring in which the wind presents frequent and serious problems and it is known to rain and even pour during its major San Isidro fair, held in the month of May. Several photographs in this book reflect perfectly an

afternoon of bullfighting in the rain in Las Ventas: one of them corresponds to May 15, 1998, precisely the day of the city's Patron Saint, San Isidro, who lends his name to this prestigious bullfight fair. It was on that date, in the midst of a drenching downpour, that José Tomás executed a truly splendid *faena*, of highly meritorious human and artistic proportions, which totally captivated his audience. This extraordinary photography has captured the Madrid matador performing in a pool of water, with rolling waves, blown along by the wind, until they crash against the wooden *barrera*. It seemed like a miracle that José Tomás was able to remain afloat without sinking, amidst so much water swirling around his feet; buoyed up solely by his own spiritual strength. It is evident that that afternoon yet another miracle was produced: it lied in the true wonder of José Tomás's *toreo* and its barest, purest form of expression.

Intimately related to the *natural* and to the *derechazo* is the *pase de pecho* — or, as it was called in the past, a "forced chest pass" —, executed with both hands, but always directed at the bull's opposite horn. It was called "forced" or "obligatory" when it was first created, because it was performed before a very strong toro, which was gaining increasingly more terrain from the torero, making it necessary for the matador to free himself from the animal's oncoming charge. He did so by sending the bull off, before it overcame him and he ended up being tossed and hurt. However, with the passage of time, the chest pass has lost its condition of "forced" in order to gain greater artistic dimension from the moment that the *diestro* imposes his own will over the bull's. That is, from the very instant in which the matador chooses when and how to end off the *naturales* and send the bull off with a high pass. As regards the "when", there is indeed no doubt: at the end of a series of *naturales* or *derechazos*; the "how" admits, as almost everything in *toreo*, a variety of interpretations, all of which are very much in accord with the personality and criteria of each torero. The chest pass can be performed with an open stance or with feet together, although the former proves to be longer and more profound, and the latter, more ethereal and superficial. In addition, the path which the torero imposes on the bull in the *pase de pecho* can be straight, semi-circular or trace a full circle, each version being different but none is better nor worse than the others.

This is where individual tastes and preferences come into play and something so undefinable as the concept or very idea of *toreo*, that which makes the torero's work longer and duller, or shorter and brighter. It is not necessary to explain that the torero is in no way obliged to end a *natural* with a *pase de pecho*, and that according to each matador and, above all, according to each bull and each moment in its *lidia*, he can conclude the series of *naturales* with a variety of other *suertes*, as we will see later on. The only obligation which does weigh over the *lidiador* heavily is that what he does, he should do well, with purity and truth, for if this is not the case, his work will be "rewarded" in the end with "silence", the harshest and most feared of all punishments: a round of jeering indicates anger, but "silence" reflects total indifference.

In the execution of the *natural*, other important elements also come into play: among them, that the torero should turn his chest towards the bull, so that he is positioned as little in profile as possible, he should advance the *muleta* in order to bring the bull along fully *toreado* or engaged in the *muleta*, and he should *cargar la suerte*, an abstract concept related to the respective terrains of the bull and the bullfighter and also to the very stance adopted by the matador in relation with the animal's charge. The assumption and putting into practize of all of these concepts are what endow *toreo* with greater truth and purity, while transmitting a sense of seduction and illusion to the public. These two concepts — truth and purity — which, even though we have repeated them over and over again, have not lost any of their validity.

Everything we have said about the *natural* can also be attributed to the *derechazo* or right-handed pass, with the only difference that in this *suerte*, the matador holds the *muleta* in his right hand, draped over the sword, which spreads it out and affords it greater extension. The *derechazo* loses its naturalness for this very reason and also because the matador does not handle the *muleta* directly, as a rigid body — the sword — has interposed itself between the hand and the cloth, and prevents the red *muleta* from falling spontaneously. Nevertheless, this circumstance does not prevent this *muletazo* from

possessing truth and beauty, because these treasures do not lie in the *muleta*, but rather in the minds and hearts of the bullfighter and the public, when perfect harmony and conjunction exist.

The *derechazo*, which is the most common *suerte* seen nowadays during a *faena*, had a somewhat twisted beginning. In fact, it had a rather bad reputation in early bullfighting, which required many years to overcome, and it is highly likely that it has still not entirely redeemed itself. Its invention was attributed to Nicanor Villalta, and since then, roughly the 1920s, it has been the object of a campaign in the press and in taurine literature to discredit and belittle it. A great deal of emphasis was placed on the lack of naturalness which is implicit in its execution, and this criticism was aimed at blaming it for the vast majority of the more evident problems affecting the Fiesta. In this crusade against the *derechazo*, there was a great deal of exaggeration and also a considerable amount of ignorance, for it is obvious that the hypothetical problems of the Fiesta (one of them being monotony, and another, a lack of truth), were not the fault of the *derechazo*, nor its inventor.

Its very name, "*derechazo*", implies a sportive, violent, abrupt *muleta* movement, as compared with the more refined names of the *suertes* ending in a diminutive form (the "*-ina*" for example, such as the *chicuelina*). It seems, then, that even its name was intended to indicate disdain for the probable brusqueness of its execution. However, the true problem lied in the fact that the *suerte* itself was confused with Villalta's original execution; it is true that in the photographs which are conserved from that epoch, the Aragón-born bullfighter is seen fighting without much grace or elegance, perhaps because neither his own *toreo,* nor that of the majority of his colleagues at the time possessed such refinement. They were rough, clumsy passes in which the man's body was strangely bent over, so that they could be executed with his feet together. Those incipient passes were still seeking their own way and the solution for doing with the right hand, what was being done so smoothly and naturally with the left, without discarding that awkward implement, which was the sword. All those individuals who criticised the *derechazo* so much, failed to see that, over the years, this pass would indeed evolve and develop in a

truly artistic manner, until it became totally assimilated alongside the *natural*. Just a few years later, with the arrival of "Manolete" and his *toreo* — and certainly even before that —, the *derechazo* no longer showed any substantial differences with the *natural*. And not only are there none in their respective forms of execution (with the sole exception of the natural fall of the *muleta* and its folds in the *natural*), nor do we notice any differences in terms of their concepts and the bullfighter's intentions when he includes them in his *faena*. Critics of the *derechazo* failed to recognise that the problem did not reside in the birth of a new *suerte*, but in its form of execution at that particular time. A different matter entirely is the abusive use often made of the *derechazo* in today's *faena*s, without a doubt due to the fact that the torero feels more comfortable and protected before the bull, in view of the greater extension of the *muleta* he offers to the animal. This is true, but the problem is not the *suerte*, innocent as all bullfighting *suerte*s are, but the use the torero may make of it.

Now that we have established that as far as the concept is concerned, the *derechazo* is identical to the *natural*: both passes make up the basis for all *faena*s, the series of *muleta*zos which give form and structure to the *toreo* with the *muleta*. Therefore, just as in the case of the *natural*, the *derechazo*'s real importance will lie in the torero's personal execution and in the degree of truth he impresses upon his work, because we should not make the mistake of thinking that all the *faena*s have a similar category and quality. Clearly, everything that is done with the bull implies enormous merit, for in any *lance* or *pase*, whether it be a fundamental one, an adornment, or a recourse, the *lidiador* is risking his life and is clearly assuming the fact that he can die at any moment, from the time the bull emerges from the pen, until it is dragged out by the mules.

Nevertheless, of the six *faena*s which normally make up a corrida, the vast majority of them are usually what we would call ordinary *faena*s, of mediocre style and beauty, sometimes due to the fact that the bull does not offer the matador the possibility of doing any better work, and at others, because the torero does not manage to connect with the seemingly favorable conditions of the animal and still others,

because neither the bull nor the bullfighter are "having their day". These are *faena*s in which the torero merely does what he has to do professionally, and even though he will never fight in a routine manner, connection is never really established between the three fundamental elements making up this Fiesta: the bull, the bullfighter and the public. They will be *faena*s "rewarded" with "silence", whistling, or even jeering, as we have seen above; *faena*s without any history, which are, in reality, the vast majority of those which are performed in any one season. However, we should make it clear that we are speaking about the substance of *toreo*, its content, both spiritual as well as artistic, which has nothing to do with its form, for even the normal and commonplace *faena*s are made up of a succession of *suertes*. There can be technically impeccable passes, which may lack spirit, charm, magic, and do not inspire any enthusiastic shouts of "*olés*", that spontaneous manifestation of approval and delight from the public in recognition of the torero's work. And it is that indifference or lack or connection between the bull and the bullfighter which will prevent the man from deriving a more personal and intimate feeling of pleasure and satisfaction from his own *toreo*.

Once the torero manages to overcome his very real physical fear, that intangible concept which is different for each torero, and which varies greatly, depending upon his mood, his self-confidence and his degree of physical preparation, then what the matador really seeks in the ring is the pleasure he derives from bullfighting. That strange and incomparable pleasure he feels, when he manages to make the bull pass his body time and time again, precisely where and when he wants it to; that strange and incomparable pleasure he feels when he is also capable of making his own body relax and abandon its nervous tension in order to enjoy what he is doing... enjoy his *toreo*. It is not easy to explain this spiritual feeling experienced by the torero, a sensation of maximum fulfillment and joy. It is often said that when a matador "*cuaja*" or rounds out a complete performance with a bull, he would not change places with anyone in the world, because there is no greater pleasure than the emotion produced by profound *toreo*. And even though we are speaking of very private, intimate feelings, which are very difficult to transmit

from one person to another, any truly knowledgeable aficionado who has witnessed a good *faena* is also capable of comprehending and experiencing in his own flesh those very same emotions. Obviously, this is the only way to explain the survival of *toreo* through successive generations of aficionados: its intrinsic ability to transmit such profound and intangible sensations. If the spectator attending a *corrida de toros* is not touched and moved by a good *faena*, and does not feel angry and frustrated by a bad one, the Fiesta would have ceased to exist a long time ago. A spectacle in which the actors and the spectators in the drama do not identify or connect with one another and do not share identical codes, nor speak the same language, would make no sense.

Bullfighting is a vehicle for transmitting emotions, which can come from a variety of sources: sometimes through aesthetic beauty, as we have already seen, and at others, through special merit. This is the true language of *toreo*, and the *suertes* of *toreo*, the different passes and *lances*, make up the syntax which helps to keep it alive. Aesthetics, and merit as well, are fundamental ingredients in the Fiesta, because frequently the *faena*s do not move the public as a result of an artistic or aesthetic emotion, but through the tremendous valor displayed by the torero, and through the evident way in which he is risking his life in order to resolve the problems presented by the bull. Clearly when the matador achieves a perfect situation in which to interlace both emotions, the aesthetic and the valiant, it is then that the *faena*s attain their true category and historical significance. However, these are the exceptions to the rule, for both components can and often are produced separately, because very few toreros are capable of combining these two profound sentiments.

And the *derechazo*, just like the *natural*, and the fundamental *verónica* and a simple adorning pass, is a key facet in this intricate framework of emotions, which we have been describing. If the *derechazo*, which we should not consider as inferior to the *natural* — merely different and not by much —, is a really good one and the torero offers all his soul and all his truth, and all the power and force of his *toreo*, then a torrent of deep sentiments will be produced, which will reach and impress the spectator.

And therein lies the very reason why aficionados go to the bullring every afternoon: with the hope of witnessing the miracle of *toreo*, even though they know deep down that on the majority of the occasions their dreams will be dashed and they will come away with an immense feeling of emptiness and frustration.

It would make no sense to go into a detailed analysis here of the many different techniques involved in bullfighting, all of those recourses which a bullfighter might employ in order to put the different *suertes* into practize. However, I do see it necessary to point out that the majority of the criticisms directed at the *derechazo* come from the use of the "*pico*" or tip of the *muleta*, a licit and acceptable technique with certain types of complicated bulls, but which should not be admitted when it is used as a measure of taking extra advantage of good, noble charging animals. In order to understand what we mean by the "*pico*" of the *muleta*, it is necessary to refer back to the basic laws of *toreo*, which traditionally indicate that the matador must offer the bull a flat *muleta*, held horizontally between the horns and presented in a slightly oblique line which extends from his right hand (or the left, if it is a *natural*) to the bull's left horn (or right, depending upon the case). Thus, the citing should be done in a "*cruzado*" or crossover manner, and directly between the horns, and not "*al hilo*", or in a straight, direct line in front of the horn closest to the matador's body. Extending the *pico* of the *muleta* means directing the tip of the *muleta* to the bull's opposite eye, or to the contrary horn, thus establishing an empty space and distance between the animal and the torero. The "*pico*" is an acceptable recourse with bad bulls and an unacceptable means of abusing the situation with noble ones; nevertheless, as is to be expected, there are exceptions to every rule, and the failure to understand the different techniques, approaches and *lidias*, always in terms of the different way each animal charges — for no two bulls are ever exactly alike —, can only lead to error. Bullfighting has its canons, but there are no fixed, nor permanent rules; the bull evolves, and with him, so does the *toreo*.

Closely related to the *derechazo* is the so-called *circular* pass, either normal or inverted, which is a pass which goes one step further in the matador's ever present attempt to extend the bull's charge as much as possible. In the *inverted circular* pass, the *lidiador* stands with his back to the animal and cites from his right side in order to execute the pass, which should trace a path as close to a full circle as possible, in order to leave the animal in the same terrain in which it first began. When the animal is cited from behind the man, but on the left side, it is called a normal *circular*, which is identical to the one just explained except for the initial citing.

When the matador is effecting a series of *derechazos*, it is very common to see him choose to finish them off with a chest pass executed with the left hand. In order to do so and "switch hands", he can pass the *muleta* behind his back or in front of him, a *suerte* which combines an adorning pass and a recourse. These passes must be considered as intermediary stages between the *derechazo* and the chest pass, and no matter how artistic and aesthetic they may turn out to be, their sole purpose is really only functional. Needless to say that when the torero wants to add a greater measure of danger to the execution of his *naturales* and *derechazos* and his chest passes with both hands, he performs them with one or both knees on the ground. Very rarely do we see a kneeling *natural* — matador Agustín Parra "Parrita" performed them brilliantly in the fifties, and now they are executed with considerable risk by Julián López "El Juli" —, although it is possible to see a matador executing his first series of *derechazos* kneeling on the sand. As in everything, abundance or abuse take away from the impact and interest of a *suerte* and so the classic toreros who rarely include kneeling *suertes* in their repertoire, cause great sensation among spectators, when they suddenly do so. In these cases, they are transmitting a clear message of their determination and desire to succeed at all cost, which is immediately received and appreciated by those seated in the stands.

138

CITING ON THE RIGHT. CÉSAR RINCÓN. "LAS VENTAS", MADRID. 22-5-1991

DERECHAZO OR RIGHT-HANDED PASS. CÉSAR RINCÓN. "REAL MAESTRANZA", SEVILLA. 26-4-1993 >

142

DERECHAZO OR RIGHT-HANDED PASS. ENRIQUE PONCE. "VISTA ALEGRE". BILBAO. 7-6-1992

DERECHAZO OR RIGHT-HANDED PASS. JOSÉ MARÍA MANZANARES. "REAL MAESTRANZA". SEVILLA. 29-4-1993 >

144

146

INVERTED CIRCULAR PASS. JESULÍN DE UBRIQUE. "REAL MAESTRANZA". SEVILLA. 30-4-1993

INVERTED CIRCULAR. ENRIQUE PONCE. GUADALAJARA. 20-9-1992 >

PASE DE PECHO OR CHEST PASS ON THE RIGHT. JOSELITO. MADRID. 17-6-1993

PASE DE PECHO OR CHEST PASS ON THE RIGHT. CÉSAR RINCÓN. "REAL MAESTRANZA". SEVILLA. 19-4-1992 >

KNEELING PASE DE PECHO OR CHEST PASS. VICENTE BARRERA. VALENCIA. 27-7-1993
CHANGE OF HANDS BEHIND THE BACK. JOSELITO. "LAS VENTAS". MADRID. 24-10-1992 >

Fundamental *toreo*, which is so limited in its classic repertoire, has, nevertheless, a very broad range of terminations. I am not going to insist upon the need for the perfect climax or finale to what has already been performed, for that point was already covered in the section on *toreo* with the cape. I will only add that just as with the cape work, a series of *naturales* can be finished off with an almost obligatory chest pass, as well as a long list of *remates* or finishing passes, which can be striking or austere, of simple or complicated execution, of the purest *torería* or superfluously colorful. In 1945, Rafael Albaicín said of the adorning passes that "they are the complement and the elegance of truth. They can, at times, be bare and be beautiful without any adornments. However, the adornment, without truth, is indeed nothing". This very serious comment made by Albaicín reinforces everything we have said up until now, that all that is done before the bull must be fully imbued with truth and purity. And the adornments, which are, in general, light and superficial, must also be true to this axiom. To perform deep *naturales* and then ruin it all when it comes time to finish off the series, because the torero was not able to hold out just one second longer, can unfortunately destroy all of the beauty he has already accomplished.

Within the broad range of *suertes* which are used as adornments and accessory passes to the more fundamental ones, there are two essential groups to be considered, if we view them from an aesthetic point of view: those which are executed at the beginning of a series of passes and those which are performed at the end. Generally speaking, they are entirely different *suertes*, although there may also be *muletazos* of identical execution which have different names, depending upon their purpose within the context of the *faena*. In this group, we can find the *trincherazo*, with the open stance or with the feet together, which will be a more or less punishing pass, depending upon how much the torero chooses to lower his hand. This *suerte* is performed with the *muleta* mounted in the right hand over the sword, directed at the bull's left horn. The *trincherazo*, which is a pass for initiating a series of *derechazos*, can also be used as a receiving pass, at the beginning of the *faena*, and it is called a *trincherilla* if it is executed with the left hand, without the aid of the sword.

Another *suerte* which is employed at this point in the *lidia* is the so-called *capeína*, which takes its name from Pedro Moya "Niño de la Capea", and can also be used as the first *muletazo* in a series of *derechazos*. In this

suerte, the torero calls the bull from a considerable distance, with the *muleta* advanced, like some kind of parapet; as soon as the animal reaches the matador's jurisdiction, he begins to *torear* on the animal's right side, but with the *muleta* inverted, thus offering the bull the back of his hand, and not the palm, as would be the case in the *derechazo*. The *litrazo*, which we have already mentioned, can also be used to initiate a *faena* or a series of *derechazos*. All of these adorning *suertes* seek not only to first attract the public's attention and draw them into the *faena*, but also to refresh the bull's charge and to incite him to attack with greater enthusiasm and impetus. The *muleta*zos which are given here, at the end of a series of *naturales* or *derechazos,* are, in every case, substitute passes for the *pase de pecho* and they serve the same function of adornment and relief, relief for both the bull as well as for the bullfighter.

Still other passes worthy of mention are the *arrucina*, created by Mexican matador Carlos Arruza, a contemporary and leading rival of "Manolete". The *arrucina* is a very risky *suerte,* resembling a *gaonera* with the *muleta*, which is held in one hand; the *ortina*, corresponding to Madrid matador Miguel Ortas, features a similar execution only in a higher form, in which the *muleta* is swept all along the bull's back; *el pase de la firma* or signature pass, created by Manuel Granero, a versatile Valencian (he was not only a torero but a talented violinist, who was killed in the Madrid bullring in 1922), is the exact counterpoint to the *trincherazo*, executed, as a result, on the bull's other horn; the *faroles*, which can also be performed at any point in the *lidia*; Victoriano de la Serna's *pase de la flores* or "pass of the flowers", baptised thus by painter Carlos Ruano Llopis in a famous painting, which he dedicated to this torero, is executed just like the *capeína*, with the only difference that it is not performed at the beginning of a series of *derechazos*, but as the finishing pass to a number of them. The list can go on and would have to include, of course, the *molinete* or windmill pass.

The *molinete*, which is so frequently used as a finishing pass for the more fundamental *suertes*, constitutes a bright and cheerful finale, loaded with depth and personality. Its execution is similar to that of the *media verónica*: the torero wraps himself up in the *muleta* and in the bull, bending at the waist and invading the space, which corresponds to the animal's natural line of charge. The *molinete* is a happy culmination, loaded

with purity and risk, because the torero, in his full rotation, loses direct sight of the bull and he will not see it again until he has made a complete turn around, and finds himself once again facing the animal, which contemplates him in amazement and hypnotised by the fact that the man has been able to make such a graceful, precise turn. The *molinete* can be executed with both hands (or with two at a time, as in the *chicuelina*, which is then called a *riverina*), standing up or on one's knees, alone or accompanied by several other *molinetes*, linked to one another, with feet together or apart... However, whatever the interpretation, as long as the torero breaks the straight line of his body at the hip — which is called a *molinete belmontino,* in honour of he who created this interpretation, Juan Belmonte — and turns about sprightly and cheerfully, he will be transmitting to the public a very clear message: that he is not only dominating the bull, but he is also capable of showing off and adorning his work before the animal, without his *toreo* losing a bit of its depth or truth.

From a purely technical point of view, regarding the orderly development of the *lidia*, the adorning *suertes* also have an important and two-fold function. First, they enable the torero to adapt himself to the specific conditions of the bull, either in high passes or low ones, as we have seen before, but always in search of greater effectiveness. And, second, they provide the necessary preparation of the bull for its death, in which the greatest aesthetic interpretation is also sought. In this way, we frequently see the *faena*s end with a linked series of adornments, intended, above all, to predispose the public to a final round of enthusiastic applause and a much desired trophy, which is the torero's ultimate goal.

Suertes which can be catalogued within these groups are, for example, the *manoletina*, invented by Victoriano de la Serna but popularized by "Manolete", who made it an obligatory finale in almost all of his *faena*s. The *manoletina* is a *muletazo,* which is executed with two hands: the right, which is the lead one and the one which marks the *toreo*, takes hold of the *muleta* and the sword; the left grasps the *muleta* cloth from behind the matador's back and accompanies the path imposed by the right. The *manoletina* is a *suerte* of great aesthetic content, which achieves its full dimension when the matador cites the bull from a profiled stance and is capable of withstanding its slow approach, thrusting his chest forward and marking the exit from behind. As it is a high

muleta pass, it possesses, in addition to its clear adorning characteristic, a two-fold, technical purpose: that of not punishing the bull any further and also that of raising its head, moments before the matador must go in for the kill.

It might also happen that at this precise moment of its *lidia*, the bull is still very strong and requires some punishing passes with the *muleta*. Then, the matador will also seek the recognition of the public, although now he must *doblarse* with the animal, giving tight but beautiful punishing passes with either hand, or even with both, in *ayudados por bajo*, aided low passes, which we will study in greater detail in just a moment. Identical to the *manoletina* is the *bernadina* — practiced by Joaquín Bernadó, the best Catalonian torero in history and now an instructor at the Madrid Bullfighting School —, which only differs in that the *muleta* is held in a reverse manner. And there are many more *suertes*; such as the austere *riverina* (of Mexican Fermín Rivera), the colourful *giraldilla*, the complex *diamantinina* (of the Portuguese diestro Diamantino Vizeu), the charming *regiomontana* (attributable to Mexicans Manolo Martínez and Eloy Cavazos), the vertical *caroletina* (of Antonio Caro, a combination of a *molinete* and a *manoletina*),... The list would indeed prove to be endless if we were to continue.

The finishing and adorning passes often find their ultimate expression in the *desplantes*, a kind of defiant stance or gesture which vary so much and are inherent and very characteristic to the individual personality of each *lidiador*. There are highly dignified and classic *desplantes*, either standing up or kneeling down (for example, the *abaniqueo* or fanning pass, which is like a taunting or pampering maneuver, performed with the *muleta* directly in front of the bull's face, or the so-called *teléfono*, which consists of leaning one's elbow on the bull's forehead, as a sign of absolute domination of the animal), and there are other, more unorthodox and "tremendista" *desplantes* (for example, when the bullfighter turns his back to the bull, or lies on the sand in front of it, or bites its horn). All of them feature the same intention: Trying to impress the public through profound *torería* or through the sensation of danger and disregard for one's physical integrity. In this latter respect, there is no difference.

TRINCHERILLA. MORANTE DE LA PUEBLA. "LAS VENTAS". MADRID. 29-5-2000

TRINCHERAZO. ARMILLITA. "LAS VENTAS". MADRID. 20-5-1993 >

164

CAPEÍNA. CRISTINA SÁNCHEZ. TOLEDO. 19-3-1993
PASE DE LA FIRMA OR SIGNATURE PASS. ESPARTACO. "REAL MAESTRANZA". SEVILLA. 29-4-1993 >

PASE DE LA FIRMA OR SIGNATURE PASS ON THE LEFT. FINITO DE CÓRDOBA. "LAS VENTAS", MADRID. 29-5-2000

MOLINETE OR WINDMILL PASS WITH THE LEFT HAND. DIEGO GONZÁLEZ. "LAS VENTAS", MADRID. 18-9-1994 >

MOLINETE OR WINDMILL PASS WITH THE RIGHT HAND. PACO OJEDA. "LAS VENTAS". MADRID. 18-5-1992

MOLINETE OR WINDMILL PASS WITH THE RIGHT HAND. NIÑO DE LA CAPEA. "LA GLORIETA". SALAMANCA. 15-9-1992 >

172

KNEELING MOLINETE OR WINDMILL PASS. LITRI. "LAS VENTAS", MADRID. 12-5-1992

MANOLETINA. VICENTE BARRERA. VALENCIA. 22-7-1993 >

MANOLETINA. JOSÉ TOMÁS. "LAS VENTAS", MADRID. 15-5-1998

MANOLETINA. LITRI. GUADALAJARA. 19-9-1992 >

Throughout our review of *toreo* with the *muleta*, we have seen that a series of *suertes* executed with both hands exist, which are performed at very different moments in the course of the *lidia*. The *ayudados* or aided passes are intended to combine two important elements: the beauty and the difficulty involved in their execution. In reality, as has been the case with the *verónica* and with the *natural*, for a professional torero it is not difficult to fight with both hands; the true difficulty lies in doing so with elegance and with a harmonious movement of both arms, for each one holds an independent element, a moving one and a rigid one, that is the *muleta* and the sword. There are a *ayudados por alto* and *por bajo* (aided high and low passes), aided passes executed at the beginning of the *faena* and at the end, serving as a caress or as a whiplash to the bull, depending upon the conditions of the animal; and there are aided passes which are executed as a consecutive series of adornments, with intentions similar to the *manoletina,* for example, the *kikirikí* — a slight *toque* or flick of the cloth before the face of the bull, with the *muleta* held at an average height —. This *suerte* was invented by the famous "Gallo" family, José "Gallito" and his brother Rafael "El Gallo", and was given such an unusual name by bullfight critic "Don Pío". We must also mention the *sanjuanera*, of Mexican Luis Procuna. The aided high and low passes must be steeped in *torería* and *temple*, because they constitute the very essence of these *suertes*: the parallel and rhythmic movement of both arms, and the magical use of the bullfighter's wrists, which should *torear* cleanly and smoothly. A great deal of truth can be found in the aided passes and also a driving desire to please the public, which participates happily and feels involved in the spirit and profound sentiment of the torero.

All of what we have described above occurred — that magical connection between the spectators and the torero, with *toreo* as the vehicle capable of transmitting the emotions — in the Madrid bullring on May 24, 1993. That afternoon, Enrique Ponce ended his *faena* with some very tight passes executed with both hands, in which he elegantly bent his leg and his very elastic, yet firm body. These were passes in which the animal was fully engaged in the folds of his *muleta*, a weightless cloth, which deceived the bull on one side and on the other, in a gentle yet resolute manner. That day, Enrique Ponce became a *"figura del toreo"*, a top star, just like José Tomás, who had ratified his category on that windy afternoon, on which he so valiantly tossed the cape behind his back; and also like Colombian matador César Rincón, when he cited the bull from afar, at a very great distance, and waited undaunted and fearless for it to charge with all its force, impetus and aggressiveness, refusing to relinquish so much as an inch of his ground and without batting an eye or raising a brow. The same can be said of many other toreros on their most glorious afternoons, those who contribute to forging that chronicle of blood and success, death and glory, which forms the very foundation for the history of *toreo*.

AYUDADO POR ALTO OR AIDED HIGH PASS. JUAN CARLOS GARCÍA. "LAS VENTAS". MADRID. 29-9-1993

AYUDADO POR BAJO OR AIDED LOW PASS. ENRIQUE PONCE. TOLEDO. 11-4-1992 >

AYUDADO POR BAJO OR AIDED LOW PASS. ENRIQUE PONCE. "LAS VENTAS", MADRID. 24-5-1993

AYUDADO POR BAJO OR AIDED LOW PASS. ENRIQUE PONCE. "LAS VENTAS", MADRID. 11-6-1992 >

The *lidia* concludes with the final, ultimate *suerte*, the so-called *suerte suprema: la estocada* (the swordthrust), the rational act of risking one's life in order to take the bull's. The "moment of truth", as it is called, is the only moment in which the matador physically attacks the bull, for all of the foregoing has been *toreo*, based on tricking, coaxing and deceiving. And it is now, at this moment, precisely when he goes into kill, that the *diestro* must put his own life on the line, with the greatest purity and honesty. When he effects this final act, he must now attack the bull, thus renouncing the right to defend himself and losing full sight of the animal's menacing head, while he allows the horns to pass just centimetres from his body. The bull dies, that is true, but it does not do so gratuitously, for the torero offers the animal the very real possibility of killing while it meets its own death.

This is the very essence of Tauromachy and what differentiates it from all the other arts and from all the other sciences, for as Orson Welles put it: "The torero is an actor to whom very real things happen". Death, its black wings, ever constant and feared, is always present and fluttering about in the approximately two hours during which the corrida lasts; death, which is more than likely for the Bull, the ultimate climax to the victory of man's intelligence over the brute force of the animal, and the always possible but never desired death of the Man, which is offered as a solemn tribute.

A young Madrid-born torero, José Cubero "Yiyo", a magnificent matador designated to occupy a prominent position in his profession, died in 1985, when his heart was sliced in two, like the wings of a dove, by a terrible goring, which even the skilled surgeon's hands could not repair. Some time before — perhaps a year or maybe just a few months —, he had declared in an interview that he preferred to die in the arena, rather than in an absurd car accident on Madrid's bustling ring road, the M-30. "Yiyo" died in Colmenar Viejo, a boy with a child's face, like a fallen angel. It was a premature death lacking in all logic, which converted him into a legend, bringing him glory and eternal recognition. Just like "Gallito", who, at twenty-five years of age, had, nevertheless, had sufficient time for everything — for fame, fortune and for crowning the Olympus of *Toreo* —, time for everything except for living his own life to the fullest. Like

"Manolete", who was called the "Monstruo", meaning "fantastic creature", who died when he was about to announce his retirement from active bullfighting, tired and bored by the endless demands of the publics. Like so many other toreros, famous and unknown, who have paid their tribute and nurtured the tree of bullfighting with their own blood.

What makes so many young people today, in the 21st century, a large number of whom are the offspring of well-to-do families who lack for nothing, give up everything with the sole goal of becoming a bullfighter? It must be for some honest, vital and transcendental cause. Beyond the fame and glory and beyond the money and luxury such a life might afford, there is only one clear goal: the desire to reach an understanding with the bull and establish an intimate connection in an arena with the force irradiated by a brave, indomitable animal, which, nevertheless, allows itself to be submitted, deceived and seduced by the intelligence and truth of a man, bared of all other elements except his wisdom, his knowledge and his courage. Is there anything purer and more noble than that struggle between the brute force and the human mind? This is precisely why *Toreo* exists today and the only way it can be justified, and for that reason spectators continue to flock to the rings. Because this is the only place where each afternoon that unique spectacle unfolds, in which Life confronts Death on equal terms, between the "last of the ancient men" — as the Portuguese Nobel prize winner José Saramago called the toreros —, and the bull, that wild and noble beast, which inhabits a tiny, marvellous corner of our Earth, called the *Planeta de los Toros*.

Translated by Muriel Feiner

ESTOCADA OR SWORDTHRUST. ENRIQUE PONCE. ALCÁZAR DE SAN JUAN (CIUDAD REAL). 5-9-1992

ESTOCADA OR SWORDTHRUST. ENRIQUE PONCE. "LAS VENTAS", MADRID. 29-5-1992 >

About the Work

The photographs for this book have been made during a period of 10 years during which Ricardo B. Sánchez has photographed over 160 bullfights in most of the important bullrings in Spain. More than 10.000 thousand images were shot to select these pictures, 98% of the material has been recorded on Fuji Velvia film and 2% on Kodachrome 64.The equipment used was Leica R4 cameras with a Tamron SP 200-500 mm lens or a Tamron SP 300 mm mounted on a Gitzo tripod. These photographs were made at speeds which range from a second to a 15th. of a second. In some cases, due to the fact that most of these photographs were made in the shade, the images have been warmed up to eliminate some excessive green and blue tones but otherwise they are true to what the camera recorded on the film.

If you want more information about the author or his work, please write to the following email address: ricardobsanchez@hotmail.com.

Acknowledgments

My thanks to all the *toreros* who appear in these photos for their art, without which this book would never have been possible; to Eugenio Niño and Antonio Suñer, who were the first to believe in this project and supported me from their respective places; to Virgilio Cano de Lope, Ambrosio Aguado Bonet and Pedro Mora for their invaluable assistance from the Community of Madrid; to the Toresma firm for their disinterested collaboration; to Eric Mosel, Andrea Tschechow and Gregor Nuser for sharing this fascination for the art of the bullfight; to Pedro Trapote for his invaluable assistance on my trips to Seville and for his passionate interest in the bullfight; to Michael Wigram for his unconditional support, his generosity and his knowledge of the *fiesta brava*; to Luciano Ruano and Santiago Olmo for their sporadic support; to José Luis Cano and his Fotosíntesis team for their painstaking care in processing my photographic work; to my friends Gilda Sobelman and Humberto Gómez for acting as talismans and helping me believe in what I did not think was possible; to my publisher Juan de Muga and the staff at Polígrafa, for making a dream cherished for 28 years come true; to Adolfo Fernández Vitorio for his unflagging support and friendship; to José Luis Ramón for his wonderful bullfighter's text, who recounts what one does and what one feels when faced by a bull in the ring; to my good friend Rosa Olivares for all the hours we have spent talking about seduction, deceit, illusion and truth; to Muriel Feiner for her elegant translation; to the team at Format Digital for their sensitivity and patience; to Pedro Carta for his sharp, valuable opinions; and to Sarah Boudreau for her patience, clear-sightedness and affectionate support. Lastly, I want to thank all those who in some way or another have contributed to making this project a reality and whose names I have absent-mindedly omitted. And I beg the pardon of all *toreros* whose art I have not reflected in this book; my anthology is not a value judgment of those who display their mastery in the ring, rather it is limited to the *toreros* I had the good fortune to watch and photograph.